Carsten Jensen

Equality

in the Nordic World

Aarhus University Press / The University of Wisconsin Press

The Nordic World
Equality in the Nordic World
© Carsten Jensen 2021

Cover, layout, and typesetting:
Camilla Jørgensen, Trefold
Cover photograph: Lars Kruse, Aarhus University
Copy editors: Heidi Flegal and Mia Gaudern
Acquisitions editors: Amber Rose Cederström
and Karina Bell Ottosen
This book is typeset in FS Ostro and printed
on Munken Lynx 130 g
Printed by Narayana Press, Denmark
Printed in Denmark 2021

ISBN 978 87 7219 326 7
ISBN 978 0 299 33414 7

This book is available in a digital edition

Library of Congress Cataloging-in-Publication
data is available

Published with the generous support of
the Aarhus University Research Foundation,
the Carlsberg Foundation, and the Nordic
Council of Ministers

The Nordic World series is copublished by
Aarhus University Press and the University
of Wisconsin Press

Aarhus University Press
aarhusuniversitypress.dk

The University of Wisconsin Press
uwpress.wisc.edu

PEER
REVIEWED

MIX
Paper
FSC FSC® C010651

Contents

Chapter 1.
Introduction

The Nordic nations are among the most equal on Earth. A larger number of ordinary people get a share of society's wealth and opportunities here than almost anywhere else. The result is not only high levels of economic equality, but also better life chances for children from disadvantaged families, more gender equality on the labor market, and reduced class differences in people's health and well-being.

If you are a fan of equality, there is much to like about the Nordics. During the last couple of US presidential election cycles, Bernie Sanders, while seeking the Democratic Party nomination, several times made statements like this:

"I think we should look to countries like Denmark, like Sweden and Norway, and learn what they have accomplished for their working people."

Such enthusiasm for the Nordics is widely shared by politicians, journalists, and laypeople. The question we must ask, then, is this: How is it possible that these societies count among both the richest *and* the most equal in existence? Is there a special recipe?

To answer this question, we first need to establish some basic facts about the Nordic experience. What precisely is the nature of the equality enjoyed by people in the Nordic countries? We may distinguish between three forms of equality that relate to three different spheres of human life: economics, gender, and youth. The Nordics stand out in all three spheres, but they do so in different ways and for different reasons.

A solid understanding of the facts is essential, not least because there are several unfounded claims circulating about the Nordic model of equality. One is that the Nordics are "socialist" or even "communist" economies. This is a big misunderstanding. There is roughly the same proportion of millionaires in Denmark, in Norway, and in Sweden as there is in the US. Although the latter hosts more of the truly super-rich, the Nordics are still home to several billionaires.

Another popular misconception is that the Nordics have a long history of equality and social harmony that may go as far back as the trading culture of the Vikings, as if, metaphorically speaking, there is some unique Nordic gene that makes people more likely to develop a social affinity with each other. As far as we can tell, this is wrong. Obviously, like all other countries, the Nordics have experienced special circumstances that shaped how they got to where they are today. However, the emergence of Nordic equality is more a result of luck than a predetermined historical outcome.

Each of the next three chapters delves into one of the contexts of equality I mentioned earlier: economics, gender, and youth. While inequality exists in other areas of life, these are the areas where the Nordics have particularly high levels of equality. I present some of the key facts about each type of equality along with an introduction to the underlying policies. For instance, in the chapter on economic equality, I outline the role of the welfare state and wage-setting institutions. After having established what we mean by "equality," I ask "how the bumblebee can fly," that is, how the Nordics are able to combine a high degree of equality with affluence. I argue that the key to success is the organization of the labor market and the educational system, which allows companies to stay competitive even though costs are high.

I also explain how the unique character of the Nordic model of equality is self-reinforcing in that, among other things, it creates a strong sense of social affinity across the population. Other noteworthy features of the Nordic countries are the electoral system, a high level of corporatism, and ethnic and religious homogeneity. Throughout the book I try to emphasize the downsides and shortcomings of the Nordic model, but towards the end I take a more thorough look at some of the graver challenges ahead, notably an increasingly top-heavy age demographic and an increasingly diverse population, which is polarizing support for social protection and income redistribution. The fate of the Nordic model of equality is far from certain.

This book concerns the experiences of Denmark, Norway, and Sweden. Strictly speaking, these are the Scandinavian countries, not the Nordic countries. The Nordic region also includes Finland and Iceland – and, depending on the level of detail, the self-governing territories of Greenland, the Faroe Islands, and Åland. However, when it comes to equality, it is in fact the Scandinavian nations that stand out, both in terms of the level of equality they have achieved (although Finland and Iceland are also in the same league) and the reasons behind their achievements. Most people outside the Nordic region probably think I am simply mincing words, but it is important to flag the issue here to avoid misunderstandings.

Chapter 2.
Economic equality

When we talk about equality, we intuitively think about money. Some have a lot, others next to nothing. Obviously, money is not the only aspect of life in which some have more than others. However, in a book about equality, this is nevertheless the natural place to begin. Money makes the world go round, as they say – and at any rate it matters greatly to the other forms of equality discussed in the subsequent chapters.

I want to start by presenting a set of facts about economic equality in the Nordics, comparing this small cluster of nations with the US and Italy. The US is known for its heavy emphasis on free market capitalism and its acceptance of sweeping inequalities. As such, it represents a very different alternative to the Nordic model when it comes to economic equality. Italy, conversely, is an archetypical example of the conservative social model of Southern Europe. As will become evident in the next chapter, this model has traditionally put heavy emphasis on the male breadwinner and the value of the traditional family structure – features which, to varying degrees, are also found in countries such as Germany, France, and Spain (Esping-Andersen 1999; Jensen & van Kersbergen 2017). The American and Italian experiences thus represent distinct alternative ways of organizing a society, highlighting the unique character of the Nordic countries.

A first look at the data

When measuring economic equality, we typically study equality of income. Most adults earn an income in one way or another. In industrialized societies, a majority of people make their living from a job; they are wage earners. Others have their own business and make an income from their company's profit. Still others earn their income from stocks, real estate, and other assets that generate a return. Finally, some get their money from pensions, unemployment benefits, or other income maintenance programs. Whatever the source, all of this is income – and not everybody has the same amount of it.

How do we estimate the unevenness in a country's distribution of income? The Gini coefficient is the best-known measure, and it is frequently used by both governments and journalists to convey an impression of the overall level of inequality in a country. The Gini coefficient calculates how much of a given country's total income would have to be redistributed to achieve perfect equality. It ranges from 0 to 1, with 0 indicating that all individuals earn exactly the same, and 1 indicating that one individual earns everything. In the real world, the Gini coefficient never approaches either 0 or 1. Even in the most equal societies, including the Nordics, some people earn more than the rest, and even in the most unequal places there are limits to how much a small clique can grab for themselves.

Figure 2.1 shows the Gini coefficient of disposable incomes for Denmark, Norway, Sweden, the US, and Italy. It is calculated for disposable income, that is, how much people have left to spend after taxes have been paid and welfare transfers received. This way the figure captures people's ability to maintain a given lifestyle. It is plainly evident that the Gini coefficient is much higher for the US and Italy than for the Nordics. Indeed, the American Gini coefficient is 33 percent higher than the combined average for Denmark, Norway, and Sweden.

Figure 2.1 Gini coefficients of disposable income

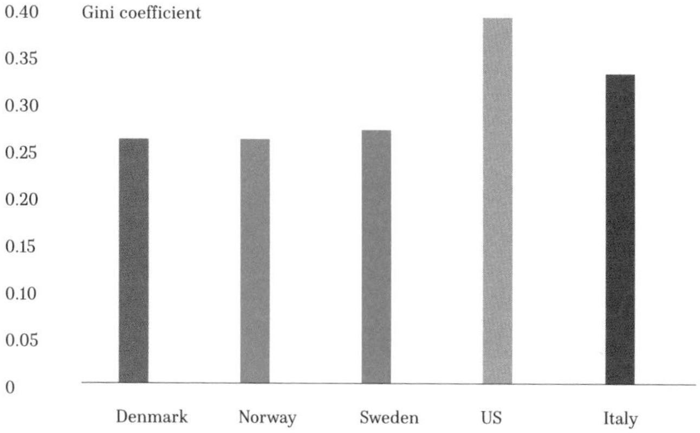

Source: OECD (2018)

The Italian Gini coefficient is situated between the low Nordic levels and the high US level. This reflects the situation across Europe, where countries such as France, Spain, and Germany also exhibit Gini coefficients significantly above the Nordic level. As I will explain later, this is a function of these countries' organization of their labor markets, which tends to create a large difference between labor market insiders (with well-paid, secure jobs) and labor market outsiders (with low-paid, insecure jobs – if they have jobs at all).

Gini coefficients are valuable for summarizing the overall level of equality in a country, but the measure suffers from at least two shortcomings. First, it is abstract. We have no intuitive understanding of what a given Gini coefficient implies. Yes, the Nordics are more equal than the US and China, but how big are the differences really? Second, it gives a single score for an entire country, but it tells us nothing about which parts of the society are causing the inequality: Is it the rich pulling away from everybody else, or is it the distance between the middle class and the poor that is increasing? For these reasons, it makes sense to supplement the Gini coefficient with so-called income ratios.[1]

Imagine lining up all the individuals in a country, starting with the poorest person and ending with the richest. Now divide the line of people into one hundred parts, each consisting of one percent of the people in the line. We can now calculate the average income for each of these hundred parts, called percentiles. Starting from the bottom, the first percentile might make $5,000 per year. At the other end of the line, the 99th percentile might make $100,000 per year. Now, it becomes possible to calculate the ratio between the incomes of these two percentiles. In this imaginary example, the ratio is 100,000/5,000 = 20, meaning that the people in the 99th percentile earn 20 times more than those in the first percentile.

Comparing the very rich to the very poor does not tell us all that much about the everyday experience of ordinary people and the societies they live in. It is therefore customary to calculate ratios based on the income of the 10th, 50th, and 90th percentiles. The 10th percentile captures the income of the poor-but-not-destitute (examples might be night-shift cleaners or short-contract farm-workers); the 50th percentile captures the income of the middle class (such as teachers and nurses); and the 90th percentile captures the income of the upper middle class (such as medical doctors and engineers). By looking at the two ratios between these percentiles, we can study the distance between the lowest-ranked wage earners and the middle class, and between the middle class and the upper middle class.

1.
For a broader introduction to measurements of equality, see Jensen & van Kersbergen (2017)

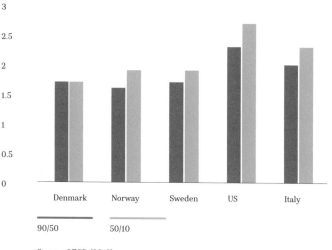

Figure 2.2 Ratios of disposable income

90/50   50/10

Source: OECD (2018)

Figure 2.2 shows the two ratios for disposable incomes in Denmark, Norway, Sweden, the US, and Italy. We can see that people in the 90th percentile in the Nordics make a little more than 1.5 times more than people in the 50th percentile; in contrast, Americans in the 90th percentile make 2.3 times more than their compatriots in the 50th percentile. Similarly, people in the Nordic countries who find themselves in the 50th percentile earn around 1.8 times more than people in the 10th percentile; in the US, the 50th percentile makes 2.7 times more than the 10th percentile. The upshot is that the distance from the bottom to the middle class is 32 percent larger in the US than in the Nordic countries, and the distance from the middle class to the upper middle class is another 28 percent larger. Italy – much like other Continental European countries such as Germany and France – once again falls in between these extremes.

15

To sum up, the Nordic countries are not only relatively equal in the general sense as measured by the Gini coefficient; they are simultaneously characterized by a short distance from the middle class to the upper class, and from the middle class to the bottom. This is not trivial. One could easily imagine a scenario where the middle class is relatively close to the well-off, but where a huge gulf separates these groups from a society's poor citizens. It is important to stress that this does *not* imply that the Nordics have obtained – or are aiming for – complete equality. Far from it. Yet it *does* mean that the Nordic countries share their affluence in a way that is largely unseen anywhere else in the world. What are the social mechanics behind this?

The model of the universal welfare state

Apart from their levels of equality, the Nordics may be best known for their welfare states. It is conventional to label these as *universal*. This means that the guiding principle, though not always the reality on the ground, is that all citizens and people with legal residence have an automatic and unconditional right to public benefits if they happen to need them – benefits that are of equal quality for all claimants and are paid for via general taxes (Esping-Andersen 1990). There are three elements to this definition.

First, such rights are automatic and unconditional. If you are jobless, sick, or old, you are entitled to benefits that (at least partly) compensate you for your income loss. The unemployed receive social assistance, the disabled receive disability pensions, and so on. If relevant, you similarly have access to treatments and services to help you: free education for the young, free hospitals for the sick and injured, care homes for the old and frail. All of this is granted as a matter of citizenship rights, meaning that because a person is a Danish, Norwegian, or Swedish citizen, they are legally entitled to such benefits.

Second, benefits are paid for via general taxes that are typically levied on people's income and consumption (so-called indirect taxes, such as value-added tax/VAT or sales tax). Unlike in many other countries, people do not have individual job-based insurance plans, or health coverage through programs dedicated to subgroups of the population, with one program for medical doctors, another for industrial workers, and so on. Instead, all citizens are members of the same health coverage program – the one run by the government.

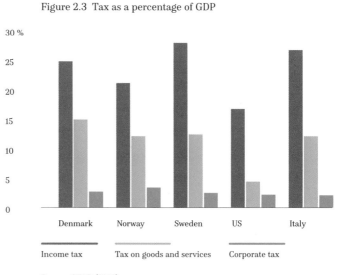

Figure 2.3 Tax as a percentage of GDP

* Note that the total tax burden includes a few small items not reflected in the figure

Income tax   Tax on goods and services   Corporate tax

Source: OECD (2018)

To get a sense of the composition of the tax burden, consult Figure 2.3. Here we can see the amount of tax levied on people's incomes, on the goods and services they buy, and, finally, on businesses. To give an impression of the size of each component, the tax burden is measured as a percentage of each country's gross domestic product

17

(GDP). The first thing to notice is that the Nordics tax much more heavily than the US. The average total tax burden is 42.5 percent in the Nordic countries, compared to just 26.3 percent in the US.

It is also evident from Figure 2.3 that what really makes the Nordic countries stand out is their taxes on income and consumption. Contrary to what some might think, the Nordic welfare states are not primarily paid for by businesses, but by the citizens themselves (Cusack & Beramendi 2006; Beramendi & Rueda 2007). Obviously, high taxes on ordinary citizens can spill over into demands for higher wages, which in turn can reduce profitability for companies. However, the wage-setting institutions of the Nordic countries make sure that the spillover is limited. As I explain below, it is a precondition for the Nordic model of equality that businesses are allowed to generate a healthy profit without being taxed out of the country.

It is noteworthy that Italy, with a tax burden of 42.9 percent of GDP, looks a lot like the Nordics in terms of the size and composition of its taxation. This reflects the fact that the Italian welfare state is very costly – as are most other Continental European welfare states, and, indeed, the Nordic ones. Overall, the Continental European welfare states create less equality than the Nordics do, and they have a number of downsides, as will be made apparent in the next two chapters. However, the price tag is roughly the same as in the Nordic countries.

The third element of universalism is that benefits are the same for all citizens. The medical doctor and the businessman are treated the same as the blue-collar worker and the waitress. This element follows directly from the second element. Since people are not members of different insurance plans or programs, they are not entitled to different benefits and services. In most other countries outside the Nordics, the rule of thumb is that those with a high income have been able to pay larger insurance premiums and are thus entitled to more than those with a low income.

It makes intuitive sense that a universal welfare state model like the one described here benefits those who have least money to begin with. No matter how much you have contributed in taxes, you receive the same treatment as everybody else. This is particularly important because the Nordics not only have generous healthcare and old-age pensions – which almost everyone, rich or poor, will very likely end up needing – but also relatively generous benefits for marginalized citizens. Social assistance, the last safety net for those with no other means of income, is considerably higher in the Nordics than in the US or the UK, for example. This means that the number of deeply impoverished people is very small in the Nordic countries.

The universal welfare state is a distinct feature of the Nordic countries with substantial equality-generating effects. Still, it is important to be aware that its universalism is only a principle, and many social programs in fact deviate from it.[2] The most important deviation is probably in the pension system. Although citizens are guaranteed a basic pension by the state, all three Nordic countries have supplemented the basic pensions with mandatory occupational pensions, as well as purely private ones (referred to as "the second and third pillars" of such pension systems). This creates substantial differences in the living standards of the elderly, depending on how much money they earned while working.

Wage setting

The welfare state and the associated taxation are important mechanisms for redistributing money from the well-off to the less well-off. However, Nordic equality is visible even before the welfare state's redistribution measures kick in. We can see this in Figure 2.4, which reports ratios of gross income, meaning people's income *be-*

2.
For a review of recent trends, see Kvist et al. (2012)

fore taxes have been paid and welfare transfers received. The ratios are calculated exactly as above, in Figure 2.2, but this time they capture the inequalities in how much people earn.

Figure 2.4 Ratios of gross income

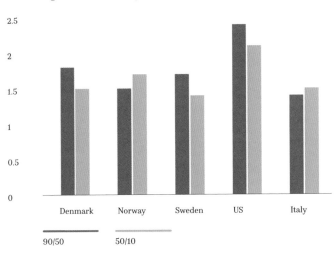

Source: OECD (2018)

The ratio between the 90th and 50th percentiles hovers between 1.5 and 1.8 in the Nordic countries, compared to 2.4 in the US. The 50th-to-10th ratios of the Nordics range from 1.4 to 1.7, compared to the American ratio of 2.1. On average, this implies that the distance from the 10th to the 50th percentile is 29 percent larger in the US than in the Nordics, while the distance from the 50th to the 90th percentile is 32 percent larger. In a nutshell, people in the Nordics do not just become equal because of the universal welfare state; they are also equal because they have equal pay to begin with.

How does this equality in earnings come about? A key explanation is found in centralized wage negotiations (Wallerstein 1999; Visser & Checci 2009). In the Nordics, collective wage bargaining normally takes place for entire sectors between the unions representing the employees and the employer associations representing the businesses. The "collective bargains" struck between these parties then apply to all employees, including those who are not members of a union. There are some exceptions to this, as some sectors and companies have decided not to participate, but for the vast majority of wage earners, collective wage bargaining is the name of the game. By 2015, 84 percent of the Danish workforce was covered by collective bargaining; in Norway the figure was 67 percent, and in Sweden 90 percent. This can be compared to around 12 percent in the US (OECD 2018).

Collective bargaining tends to compress wages. While the wage deals made by the unions and employer associations in recent years have allowed for individual top-ups based on performance and qualifications, the general rule is that everyone working in a specific occupation earns the same. All nurses with ten years' seniority make virtually the same as similarly experienced schoolteachers, metalworkers, and so on. An employer may know Suzanne is better at her job than John is at his, but both will, in all likelihood, earn almost exactly the same pay anyway. The employer's ability to reward Suzanne will typically be more or less symbolic. This is a shame for Suzanne, but it is obviously good for equality.

Chapter 3.

Gender equality

For several decades now, Nordic women have been working almost as much as men. Women's participation in the labor market has freed them economically because they earn their own incomes, but it has also fostered what might reasonably be dubbed "a culture of gender equality." Among industrialized nations, Denmark, Norway, and Sweden are beacons of gender equality. This does not mean that perfect gender equality has been achieved, yet given how entrenched gender biases have been historically, and still are in many places, it is nevertheless a major achievement.

Front-runners

By most international rankings, the Nordics are front-runners in the field of gender equality. The United Nations Development Programme, for instance, calculates a so-called Gender Inequality Index that summarizes information about female status in terms of health (mortality rates, and teen pregnancy and birth rates), empowerment (females with at least a secondary-level education, and the female share of parliamentary seats), and labor market (female labor market participation). On this UNDP index, the Nordics routinely score very high, and they are nearly always among the ten best performers in the world. The Gender Inequality Index is meant to capture the big picture. Obviously, among affluent nations figures such as mortality rates, teen births, and the proportion of women with secondary schooling may be less informative in terms of gender equality than they may be for, say, less wealthy African nations or India. Other indices have therefore been constructed with more fine-grained data pertaining exclusively to the Western world, and here too the Nordics come out on top.[3]

What does this gender equality imply, more precisely? In the context of an affluent region, the core element is "female labor market participation" and the associated economic independence of women. To get a sense of the magnitude of Nordic women's participation in the labor market, consult Figure 3.1, which shows the percentage of males and females between 15 and 64 years old in the workforce (meaning they either have a job or are actively looking for one). Along with Denmark, Norway, and Sweden, the figure also reports the numbers for the US and Italy. The US, as in the last chapter, represents a distinctly different model compared to the Nordics when it comes to economic gender equality, whereas Italy is an archetypical example of the conservative social model found in most of Continental Europe.

The conservative social model has historically been characterized by a strong emphasis on the value of the traditional family structure, with a male breadwinner and a female homemaker (Lewis 1992; Esping-Andersen 1999). Even today, this value is clearly manifested in comparatively low female labor market participation rates. Sweden is the absolute front-runner with a female participation rate of almost 80 percent, which is less than four percentage points below that of Swedish men. In Denmark and Norway, more than 75 percent of women are in the workforce, compared to around 80 percent of men. With 67 and

3.
See, e.g., European Institute for Gender Equality (2018)

55 percent, respectively, the American and especially the Italian rates pale in comparison. The gender gap swells to 12 percentage points in the US and 20 percentage points in Italy.

Figure 3.1 Labor market participation rates

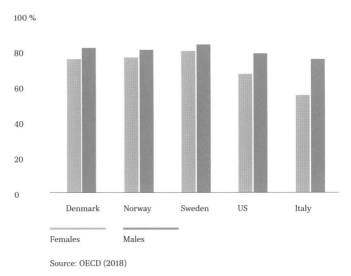

Source: OECD (2018)

Figure 3.2 breaks down these participation rates for women by age cohorts. In the Nordics, women join the labor force at high rates in their early 20s, as in the US. However, while participation rates increase even further in the Nordic countries as many young women finish university, they level off in the US, albeit at a rather high level. In Italy, these participation rates only approach (but never reach) Nordic levels for women in their late 30s and 40s. Effectively, this illustrates the fact that many Italian women only enter the labor market after their children are old enough to begin school (or preschool, if available). I will return to this point shortly.

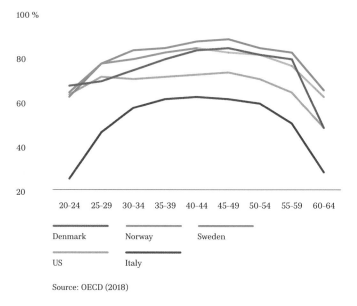

Figure 3.2 Labor market participation rates by age cohort

100 %

80

60

40

20

| 20-24 | 25-29 | 30-34 | 35-39 | 40-44 | 45-49 | 50-54 | 55-59 | 60-64 |

Denmark   Norway   Sweden

US   Italy

Source: OECD (2018)

Yet the issue at stake is not simply whether women work or not; it is also how much they get paid. Figure 3.3 displays the gender pay gap. The gender pay gap is defined as the (unadjusted) difference between the median earnings of women relative to the median earnings of men. It provides a crude but telling impression of how much money women earn compared to men. The data refer to full-time employees and self-employed individuals (note that these data are missing for Denmark). Across all five countries, female earnings are lower than male earnings, but with very substantial differences among countries. The gap for self-employed people is particularly visible, at more than twice the size in the US and Italy as it is in Norway and Sweden. The pay gap for full-time employees is five percentage points larger in the US than in the most unequal Nordic country, Sweden. Italy exhibits a small pay gap. This should, however, be viewed in the context of Italy's much lower participation rates. Those who are particularly inclined to stay out of the labor market are those with the least education, and, all else being equal, this raises the average skills level (and thus the earning capacity) of the remaining group of women who are actually in the workforce.

Figure 3.3 Gender pay gap

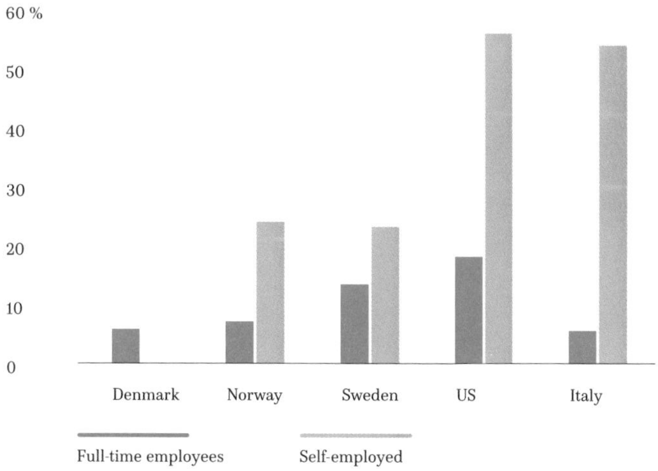

60 %
50
40
30
20
10
0

Denmark   Norway   Sweden   US   Italy

Full-time employees   Self-employed

Source: OECD (2018)

Policies

Throughout recorded human history, the family has been the primary economic unit. First and foremost, it is within the family that people have pooled and shared their resources – food, shelter, money, and so on – in order to secure the survival of the individual and the rearing of future generations. Since the industrial revolution, the typical organization of the family has followed "the male breadwinner model," where the husband earned the family's income on the labor market while the wife took care of the children and ran the household. In many parts of the world, including North America and Europe to a certain extent, this remains the dominant family model today.

The great advantage of the family as an economic unit is that it is normally tied together by emotional bonds that cause its individual members to commit to the greater good of the unit. People are willing to pool their resources even if they themselves have to forego something in the process. The downside is that the individual members become dependent on the family for their livelihood. In societies where the economy revolves around the family-as-unit, not having one can be a serious problem. This, in turn, makes family members dependent on the goodwill of the (male) head of the family. Almost invariably, a family-based economy therefore entails that women are subordinate to their husbands or to some other male patriarch.

Since the 1960s and 1970s, the Nordics have pursued a strategy of "de-familization." This means they have tried to make individuals less dependent on their families for their livelihoods. Effectively, this involves ensuring that all adult family members have jobs and earn their own money. Given its historical starting point, this policy has predominantly benefited women. Other nations also have family policies, but they typically re-emphasize the importance of the family.[4]

De-familization is the product of various policies, but the most important is undoubtedly publicly sponsored childcare. Without childcare, mothers almost always need to leave their studies or jobs to take care of their offspring. On the other hand, with childcare – and assuming that parental leave policies are in place – mothers are able to return to their previous job faster. This makes career breaks shorter and employers more likely to hire women in the first place. Training a new employee often costs a lot of money for an employer, so if there is a substantial risk that young women will leave and only return several

4.
For recent in-depth discussions of these country clusters and the associated policies and outcomes, see, e.g., Jensen (2008) and Lohmann & Zagel (2016)

years down the road, hiring them can end up being a bad financial decision.

Figure 3.4 Childcare coverage for children 0-2 years old

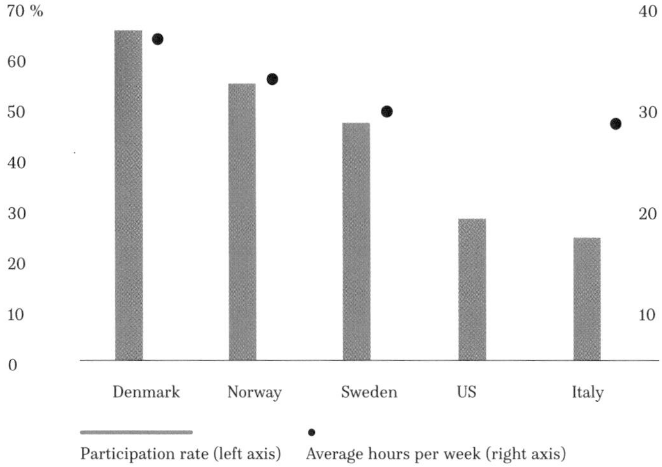

Participation rate (left axis) — Average hours per week (right axis)

Source: OECD (2018)

Figure 3.4 displays some information on childcare coverage for children below the age of three. The bars show the percentage of all children in the age cohort who are enrolled in childcare (left y axis); the black dots represent the average number of hours that the enrolled children spend in childcare per week (right y axis). Note that there is no comparable information on the average hours spent in childcare per week in the US.

Obviously, the most notable feature is the high level of participation in all three Nordic countries. An average of 55 percent of the cohort attend childcare. This number would increase significantly if we zeroed in on those aged more than six months, which is when toddlers start enrollment. This average should be compared with 28 and 24 percent in the US and Italy, respectively. The number of hours children spent in daycare facilities per week in the Nordics is, on average, more than 33, compared to 29 in Italy. This means that not only are more children enrolled in childcare programs in the Nordics, they also stay there longer every day.

Although all three of these Nordics stand out, Denmark is clearly in the lead. That makes it a good example of widespread de-familization via childcare. Enrollment rates are almost 90 percent for one-to-two-year-olds and 98 percent for three-to-five-year-olds (Statistics Denmark 2015). The Danish system is heavily subsidized, but childcare is not free of charge. The monthly fee for a child to attend a local nursery school is typically about 480 US dollars, depending on the municipality. However, parents with smaller incomes pay a reduced fee. The fact that childcare is not free emphasizes how ingrained the notion of women working has become: Very few parents even consider *not* enrolling their children in a daycare program.

In addition to comprehensive childcare arrangements, the Nordics have generous parental leave policies. Although to some extent these may be a double-edged sword, as I explain later in this chapter, the way maternity leave is organized in the Nordics also helps women balance work and family life. Essentially, Nordic paid parental leave is relatively short but generous, especially in Denmark and Sweden. As a consequence, families are able to maintain their lifestyles for the comparably brief period the woman is not working. In combination with virtually all-encompassing childcare, this means having a baby disrupts women's careers much less than it does elsewhere in the world.

Figure 3.5 summarizes the fiscal burden of all this de-familization. The figure reports public spending on family benefits as a percentage of GDP. It is plain to see that the Nordics are very different from the US and Italy. The three Nordics we see here all spend between 3 and 3.5

percent of GDP on family benefits, whereas Italy spends a moderate 2 percent and the US just 1 percent. If we look behind the numbers, the fact that Italy spends approximately twice as much on family benefits as the US also points to an interesting distinction between countries adhering to the conservative social model, such as Italy, and countries that are more plainly free market capitalist, like the US.

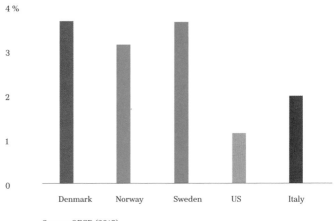

Figure 3.5 Public spending on family benefits as a percentage of GDP

Source: OECD (2018)

Countries adhering to the conservative social model are not averse to public spending on the family, but they use their family policies to protect the traditional family structure. One common way of doing this is to refrain from establishing comprehensive childcare, which saves a lot of money, and this makes the Nordics stand out, as is evident in Figure 3.5. Another way is to pay out generous family allowances or give tax breaks to families with a stay-at-home mother. Through these policies, governments can make it more attractive for families to stick to the "male breadwinner template," because some or all of these benefits would be lost if the woman started working. In the conservative social model, the public effectively subsidizes homemakers.

Yet governments are not the only source of gender bias. Workplace arrangements, when seen more broadly, can also play a part. Figure 3.6 illustrates this point. It shows the percentage of women in jobs with flexible working hours. In Italy, almost 75 percent of employed women are in jobs where working hours are set entirely by the employer. This should be compared with the 35–40 percent of employed women in such jobs in the Nordics. Here, large segments of the female (and male) workforce are able to adapt their working hours either partially or entirely. Needless to say, this sort of flexibility has a great bearing on people's ability to balance the requirements of work and family life.

Figure 3.6 Percentage of female workers with flexible working hours *

* Note that data for the US is missing

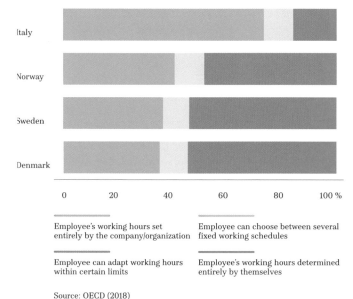

Employee's working hours set entirely by the company/organization

Employee can choose between several fixed working schedules

Employee can adapt working hours within certain limits

Employee's working hours determined entirely by themselves

Source: OECD (2018)

32

Shortcomings

Having heaped praise on the Nordic model, it is only fair to point out some of its shortcomings. As in the case of economic equality, the Nordics may be front-runners, but full gender equality is still a long way off. For instance, Figure 3.4 revealed that significant earnings gaps still exist. It is similarly well-established that women remain underrepresented in management positions, not least in the private sector.

Several scholars have pointed out that the lack of full gender equality can be explained, at least in part, by the selfsame policies that have helped foster de-familization (Mandel & Semyonov 2005; 2006; Gupta et al. 2008). This is also known as "the welfare state paradox." The explanations take slightly different angles, but the gist is that generous family benefits have two unintended consequences. First, although paid parental leave is of moderate length, at least compared to other European countries, women can still be absent from their jobs for a substantial period of time. In Denmark, for instance, total leave may be up to a year, although benefits during a long leave are comparatively modest. If a woman has two or three children, she may experience a total of three years of career interruption, and this will typically occur in her late 20s to mid-30s, a decisive period for most people's career trajectories. When women finally return to full speed, their male colleagues will often have a couple of years' head start.

Second, back when Nordic women began joining the labor force, from the 1960s onwards, they frequently found jobs in the expanding public sector as nurses, teachers, and caregivers. In a sense, this was a virtuous circle. The public sector offered both the childcare and the jobs (which often involved *working* in childcare) that women needed to enter the labor market – which in turn reinforced the need for more childcare and other family benefits. However, as a result of this virtuous circle, many occupations have become "gender ghettos." Education, childcare, eldercare, and nursing are all highly feminized. Since these are also relatively low-paying sectors, this occupational segmentation is a major cause of the gender pay gaps observed in Figure 3.3. Nordic women are rarely overtly discriminated against when it comes to pay; they frequently just happen to work in sectors that pay less than the sectors where men tend to work. Add to this the partial persistence of traditional family roles, with the female partner often working fewer hours to juggle home and family responsibilities, and you have the recipe for perpetuating gender gaps in earnings.

In brief, although the de-familization of the Nordics has been highly successful from the perspective of ensuring economic independence for women, it comes at a cost. While researchers debate the size of this cost (Korpi et al. 2013), they no longer dispute its existence. As such, this is a fine example of some of the built-in challenges of the Nordic model of equality, a topic I will return to later.

Chapter 4.
Generational equality

Today, generational inequality is one of the biggest sources of discontent and social upheaval. If too many young people are left with limited prospects for the future because older generations have pulled up the social and economic ladders they climbed themselves, this can create disillusionment and even unrest. Therefore, making sure younger generations get off to a good start in life is one of the main tasks of any responsible government. Few countries are better at this than the Nordics. Here, education is a focal point, because in modern societies the education you get will, by and large, determine what job you get, and consequently affect where you end up in the social hierarchy. However, good education opportunities are not enough if the labor market is too rigid to give young people access to decent jobs. Here, too, the Nordics are among the front-runners (Iversen & Stephens 2008; Chevalier 2016; OECD 2016; 2017; Jensen & van Kersbergen 2017).

Achievement

Figure 4.1 begins by displaying the percentages of people aged 25-34 and 55-64, respectively, with a tertiary education (meaning they hold an academic degree from a college or university). This gives a rough impression of the general level of education in a society. In the Nordic countries, almost 50 percent of people between 25 and 34 years of age have a tertiary degree, which is comparable to the American rate and almost twice the rate in Italy. It is also noteworthy that the percentage of people with a tertiary degree is around 50 percent higher in the younger cohort (25-34) than in the older cohort (55-64). This reflects a massive investment in education in the Nordics, which has boosted tertiary-level enrollment rates dramatically in recent decades.

As I explain briefly below, these high rates of tertiary education should be seen in conjunction with the comprehensive upper-secondary vocational training programs that offer young people an alternative pathway to relatively well-paid jobs. The Nordic vocational training systems combine extensive school-based teaching with apprenticeships. This sets them apart from more traditional vocational training, which is overwhelmingly industry-based. In this sense, Figure 4.1 underestimates the educational level of young Danes, Swedes, and Norwegians because many receive training and earn qualifications outside the college and university system.

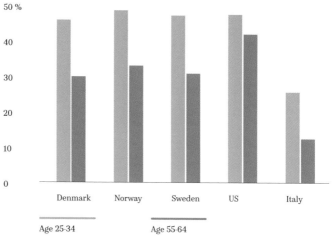
Figure 4.1 Proportion of citizens with a tertiary degree

Age 25-34   Age 55-64

Source: OECD (2018)

For young people, the main alternative to getting an education is starting work. Even so, a major problem around the world has been the rising number of NEETs, an acronym used for young people who are "not in education, employment, or training." This group, often very marginalized, has a high risk of becoming permanently stuck on the fringes of the labor market. Figure 4.2 conveys an impression of the extent of this problem for 20-24-year-olds, which make up the cohort that typically finished high school and, by that age, ought to have a job or begin tertiary education. The data is broken down by gender.

In the three Nordic countries, NEET rates hover around 10 percent; female rates are around two percentage points lower than male rates. In all likelihood, some of these young people are voluntarily neither working nor studying. Perhaps they are backpacking around the world – a highly valued activity in recent decades for many high-school graduates. Still, some fraction of the Nordic NEET rate reflects the fact that some young people never find a foothold in school or work, which will continue to hurt this particular group as they grow older. That said, compared with the NEET rates in the US and, not least, in Italy, the Nordic rates are very low. Among American youth, 14 percent of males and 16 percent of females are NEETs; in Italy, the numbers are 33 percent for males and 32 percent for females. Ten years down the road after the Great Recession of 2008, the Italian NEET rates remain shockingly high. One consequence has been massive emigration to better-off countries in Europe and North America. Since 2008, at least 1.5 million Italians, predominantly young, have left Italy (Financial Times 2017).

Figure 4.2 Percentage of people aged 20–24 who are not in education, employment, or training (NEET)

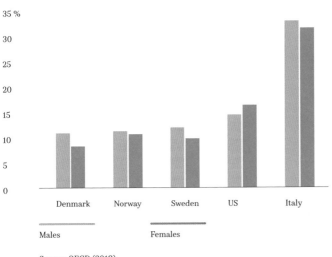

Source: OECD (2018)

For a final illustration, we may turn to educational mobility, that is, how strongly correlated the education of parents is with that of their children. How likely is it that a young person will end up in the same life situation as his or her parents? Figure 4.3 shows the educational outcome for those 25–44-year-olds for whom neither parent attained an upper-secondary education (meaning they did not graduate from high school). We can say that educational mobility is low if parents with little education tend to have children who also end up with little education. In contrast, educational mobility is high if children of parents with a low level of education tend to end up with a high level of education. Note that for presentational reasons the figure leaves out the third category, which is the middle category of upper-secondary education.

By this measure, it is clear that the Nordics boast more educational mobility than both the US and Italy. In the Nordic countries, approximately 26 percent of children with less-educated parents end up, themselves, with less than an upper-secondary education (meaning less than a high-school diploma). In the US and Italy, the corresponding percentages are 34 and 54, respectively. These high numbers should be seen in conjunction with the very low percentage of such children who end up with a tertiary education. In the Nordics, an average of 27 percent of these children get a tertiary education, compared with eight percent in both the US and Italy. Because relatively few Italians get a tertiary education in the first place, a rate of eight percent for this particular group is not dramatically worse than the rates for other groups. However, in the US, where a greater proportion of the population has a tertiary education, eight percent signifies a major mobility gap.

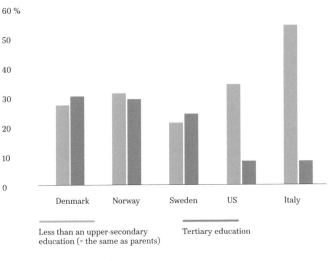

Figure 4.3 Educational outcomes of 25-44-year-olds for whom neither parent attained upper-secondary education

Less than an upper-secondary education (= the same as parents)   Tertiary education

Source: OECD (2018)

In sum, the preceding three figures exemplify how the Nordics have been able to integrate younger generations into their countries' social and economic life. The majority of young people living in Denmark, Norway, or Sweden have a reasonable chance of securing a good education or job, and talented children from disadvantaged families have a high likelihood of ending up in a better life situation than their parents. It is important to stress that this does not imply that educational mobility is anywhere near perfect; parents' backgrounds still play a major role in the life prospects of children in the Nordics. The daughter of a Swedish lawyer has a much greater likelihood of becoming a lawyer herself than the son of a blue-collar worker or a cleaning lady. Nevertheless, compared to the situation in most other places around the world, the Nordic countries have come far.

Policies

One main reason why the Nordics are able to generate relatively high levels of educational mobility is the design of their educational systems.[5] One core feature is that almost all education is free of charge. From primary school to doctoral studies, there are no tuition fees. Primary and secondary education is free almost everywhere around the world, although private options are frequently used by those who can afford them. What sets the Nordic countries apart is their sustained investment in high-quality, all-encompassing schooling, where everyone is offered the same free education opportunities from childhood and into adulthood.

Another feature that typifies the Nordic model of education, besides low or no cost for users, is the limited "tracking" or "sorting" of children. In many European countries, children are segregated at an early age according to an assessment of their academic potential. So, even though tertiary education may be free of charge in their country, a child's academic abilities as demonstrated at the tender age of, say, 11 or 12 will have a major impact on their chances of ever getting admitted to a university. In other countries, such as the US, tracking often takes the form of parents' ability to pay for private schools and universities, where the quality of teaching tends to be markedly higher than in the state-run school system.

A third central feature of Nordic education is the vocational training system all these countries use. As mentioned previously, this vocational system is school-based, which means that students combine traditional schooling with periods of hands-on apprenticeship. This ensures a high and uniform quality of vocational training and provides young people with a broader skill set than if they were to do most of their training at a single company. What is more, as a direct consequence of this, in the Nor-

5.
This section draws on Iversen & Stephens (2008), Chevalier (2016), OECD (2017), and Jensen & van Kersbergen (2017)

dic countries people with vocational certificates are able to demand higher salaries than people with similar certificates elsewhere. Simply put, to their employers, they are worth a bigger paycheck.

As a result of these features, the distribution of skills among the Nordic population is comparatively equal. Even people without tertiary degrees will often have received enough high-quality training to earn a reasonable wage. This tendency is reinforced by the representative wage negotiations or "collective bargaining" discussed in Chapter 2. However, the underlying reason why employers are able to pay decent wages to people with relatively little education is that the employees are worth their pay – a point I will return to in the next chapter. For now, consult Figure 4.4, which displays the wage differences between people with less than an upper-secondary education and those with a tertiary education, comparing both groups to people with just an upper-secondary education. On average, people with a tertiary education earn 25 percent more in the Nordics than people who just have an upper-secondary education – compared to 74 percent in the US and 41 percent in Italy. This means that the "wage premium" for getting a tertiary education is around three times larger in the US than in the Nordics. Conversely, the "wage penalty" for not having an upper-secondary education is approximately the same in the US (23 percent) as it is in the Nordics (20 percent), while it is considerably larger in Italy (32 percent).

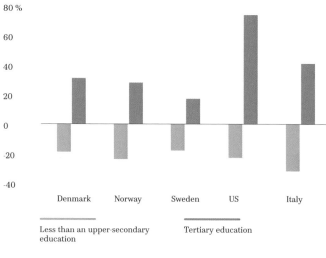

Figure 4.4 Relative earnings compared to earnings of upper-secondary school graduates

80 %

60

40

20

0

-20

-40

Denmark   Norway   Sweden   US   Italy

Less than an upper-secondary education

Tertiary education

Source: OECD (2018)

Besides the structure of the educational system, the labor markets in the Nordics are also relatively welcoming of new, young entrants. Details of the Nordic labor markets will be the topic of the next chapter, but here I would like to highlight one aspect of particular importance in the context of generational equality, namely the comparably relaxed employment regulations. It is easier for firms in the Nordic countries to fire employees in the event of a downturn or shift the precariously employed young outsiders to other tasks or jobs.

Chapter 5.

Combining equality and affluence

Although far from perfect, the Nordics are characterized by levels of economic equality, gender equality, and generational equality that are basically unparalleled. But how does all this equality fit in with the realities of the modern, globalized economy? How are Nordic countries able to pay for it all?

This chapter probes the economic underpinnings of equality. It takes issue with a notion that is widespread among pundits and politicians: that high equality leads, by necessity, to low economic growth and affluence. This "trade-off hypothesis" is wrong. Equality does not mean poor economic performance. However, this does not imply that equality will automatically foster economic growth. Rather, the relationship between equality and growth is highly complex, and it is conditional on the way a country has organized its labor market, its welfare programs, and its way of life more broadly speaking. There is no simple formula for success.

Myth-busting

Foreigners can hardly be blamed for reflexively thinking that the Nordics must be socialist economies. Surely only socialism would allow the amount of redistribution – taking money from the rich and giving it to the poor – that goes on here? As it happens, this is a misconception. The Nordic countries are all capitalist market economies, and firms and individuals often make hefty profits. We have already seen in Chapter 2 how people in the 50th percentile make around 1.5 times more than people in the 10th percentile, whereas those in the 90th percentile make another 1.5 times more than those in the 50th percentile – after tax, that is.

Another way of conveying this point is to consider how large a proportion of the population has a fortune worth more than one million US dollars. The bars in Figure 5.1 show the percentage of the population with a personal net worth of this magnitude in 2016 (and they refer to the y axis on the left). It is immediately evident that the Nordics are, on average, similar to the US and far above Italy, with the partial exception of Sweden. Two major sources of this personal wealth are home ownership and pension savings, both of which are quite widespread among middle-class families. Among the middle-aged and "soon-to-retire" group, mortgages have been paid, and pension savings have accumulated over many years. To a certain extent, then, these figures demonstrate that even ordinary families can accrue substantial amounts of wealth – even in countries with heavy tax burdens.

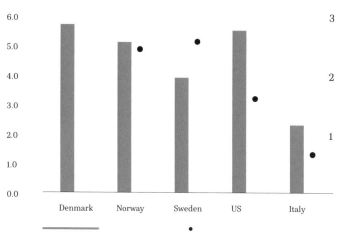

Figure 5.1 Proportion of millionaires and billionaires (in US dollars)

Percentage of population with wealth above 1 million US dollars (left axis)

Billionaires per 1 m inhabitants (right axis)

Sources: Credit Suisse (2016); Forbes Magazine (2018)

To emphasize this point, consider the black dots in Figure 5.1. They indicate the number of dollar billionaires per million inhabitants in a country. The US is home to a huge number of billionaires, more than 500 by the measure used here. However, the US population is very large, meaning that the relative number of billionaires is actually lower than the Norwegian and Swedish numbers (data for Denmark is missing). That said, the average billionaires in Norway or Sweden are less wealthy than their American colleagues. Almost all of the world's richest people – Jeff Bezos, Bill Gates, and Mark Zuckerberg, to name a few – are American, and men, and many times wealthier than "ordinary" billionaires from the Nordic countries. According to *Forbes Magazine* (2018), in 2018 the richest Norwegian was worth $6.6 billion, compared to the richest American, whose net worth was $112 billion. Indeed, a large part of the inequality found in the US is caused by the emer-

47

gence of a class of ultra-rich people who have accumulated personal fortunes so vast that by comparison they dwarf the millionaires, and even many other billionaires.

Of course, the argument here is *not* that the Nordics and the US are similar in terms of inequality. The US *is* much more unequal than any of the Nordic countries, where the equality I have described relates to all aspects of income distribution. As we saw in Chapter 2, the distances between the lowest earners (the 10th percentile) and the middle and upper middle classes (the 50th and 90th percentiles, respectively) are larger in America than in the Nordic countries. In addition, according to most definitions of personal wealth, there are no ultra-rich people in Denmark, Norway, or Sweden. Rather, what I would argue is that the Nordic model of equality does not preclude people who make an extra effort or have a special talent from earning a correspondingly high monetary reward. If you decide to complete a long university education and get a job with a law firm as an attorney, you will earn much more than, say, your friends who choose to work as shop assistants – and if you are fortunate and talented enough to become a partner in the law firm, or the managing director of a private company, you may well end up a millionaire.

Still, an oft-heard proposition is that high levels of equality demotivate people and erode thrift. If we do not have to fear poverty, why make an effort? In the interest of staying on topic I will not delve into the psychology of work ethics here. For now, I will simply look at the final outcome, where the conclusion is straightforward: There is no clear, unconditional link between a country's level of equality and its economic growth or affluence.[6]

Figure 5.2 shows GDP per capita in US dollars for the year 2016. When we compare countries, we need to correct for different levels of purchasing power. For instance, a dollar will buy you more in Italy than in the US.

6.
For recent research supporting this conclusion, see Thewissen (2014) and Neves et al. (2016)

Thus, a dollar earned in the US ought to count for less than a dollar earned in Italy when comparing the wealth of the average American and the average Italian. Therefore, the standard procedure when comparing countries is to use the so-called purchasing power parity, which weighs the value of the dollar according to a specific "basket of goods." This allows us to compare the affluence of countries without the comparison being distorted by their different price levels.

At any rate, Figure 5.2 shows that the American GDP per capita of $57,600 is indeed quite high. The average American is well off by any standard, although naturally the variance around that average is also large (hence the high inequality). Importantly, the Nordics are in the same league. Norway even beats the Americans with its GDP per capita of $58,800, while Denmark and Sweden both lag behind at around $49,000. Italy, which is more unequal than the Nordics, lags behind all the Nordics at $38,400. This underlines a crucial point: Whether or not a country is equal tells us little about its level of affluence as measured by GDP per capita. Whatever the exact method of ranking, the Nordics invariably belong to the world's most affluent nations – alongside highly unequal nations such as the US, Singapore, and the UK.

Figure 5.2 GDP per capita

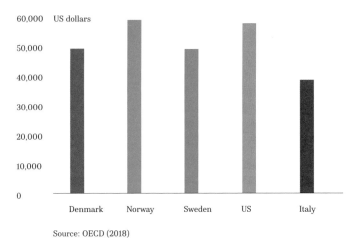

Source: OECD (2018)

Figure 5.3 Yearly growth in GDP per capita (1970 = Index 100)

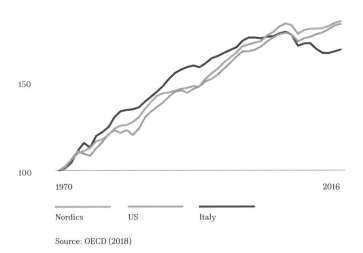

Source: OECD (2018)

The *level* of affluence is one thing; another is the *growth* in that level over time. It is possible that the Nordics are rich because of past achievements, but that things have slowed down since. Figure 5.3 investigates this proposition. It shows yearly growth in GDP per capita corrected for inflation since 1970. The year 1970 is used as the baseline year for the index, enabling us to focus on how much *more* affluent countries have become since then. For presentational reasons, the three Nordic countries are shown as one group average. This hides the fact that not all of these countries have experienced similar rates of growth at the same time. However, since we are interested in the Nordics as a whole, the grouping is justifiable. It is quite clear from this figure that all of the countries shown are roughly on the same track, although Italy has shown a worrying tendency towards slow growth over the past decade or so.

In short, there is little evidence to confirm the trade-off hypothesis, at least not in the direct sense that equality depresses growth and affluence. However, one related interpretation of the hypothesis could be that equality is fiscally irresponsible. Equality may not stop countries from becoming wealthy, but surely it must bury their governments under mountains of debt? The short answer is no, it does not. Figure 5.4 documents this, as it shows the amount of public debt (at all levels of government: local, regional, and national) measured as a percentage of GDP. We can observe two striking things here. First, public debt in the Nordics is less than half the American level, and only a third of the Italian level. Second, from 1995 to 2016, public debt decreased in Denmark and Sweden, while remaining low and stable in Norway. By comparison, in the US and Italy, debt virtually exploded. In recent years both these countries have been dangerously close to bankruptcy because of their inability to rein in public spending.

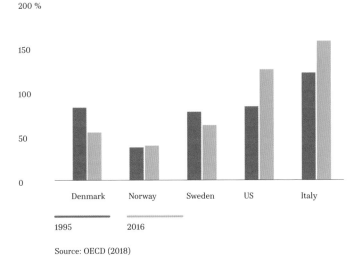

Figure 5.4 Public debt as a percentage of GDP

200 %

150

100

50

0

Denmark Norway Sweden US Italy

1995   2016

Source: OECD (2018)

There is actually a straightforward explanation for this paradox, namely, the different tax burdens, which I discussed in Chapter 2. The Nordics tax heavily, whereas the US does not. Yet while the American welfare system is small, it is *not* non-existent (Social Security and Medicare, for instance, are two popular and expensive public programs), and the American government has many other expenses as well, including its military, police, prisons, and so on. The result is that the US government simply spends more than it collects in taxes, which accumulates into mounting public debt. The Italian story is largely the same: too many government commitments and too little in taxes, given these commitments. Coupled with the low growth rates of the past decades, this has led to an explosion of public debt.

For several decades now, the Nordics have displayed a remarkable degree of fiscal responsibility. They have reined in public spending and debt, making their public finances some of the most consolidated in the world. Part of what has made this possible is a willingness to tax heavily, and this is precisely the point: You cannot have your cake and eat it too. If a country wants to pursue fiscally responsible equality, it will have to impose a heavy tax burden. Whether or not such high taxes are a price worth paying is, of course, another matter altogether – and a question that a country's citizens and politicians must decide. Clearly, the Nordic tax burden has not hampered growth, but many individuals are undeniably taxed very heavily. As I explain later, this has made taxation one of the hottest political issues on the agenda in all three Scandinavian countries and throughout the Nordic region.

How can the bumblebee fly?

Many people have compared the Nordic model of equality with a bumblebee: This insect is very bulky, and technically its wings are too small for it to fly – but nevertheless, fly it does. The Nordic model of equality is expensive, and yet it manages to create economic growth. As with the bumblebee, it is fair to ask: How is this possible?

Here, I will highlight three aspects of Nordic societies that help these bumblebees to fly: the organization of the labor market into a *flexicurity system* that allows firms to compete on international markets; a business-friendly environment with *limited red tape*; and high levels of *social trust* that make cooperation easier.

Earlier in this book we touched on all of the aspects that, taken together, constitute the flexicurity system. The word itself is a portmanteau of "flexibility" and "security." It designates a system in which employment regulation is comparably lenient – making it easy for firms to adjust to market changes by firing employees – in combination with an all-encompassing welfare state. The welfare state's role is twofold: It provides protection against the income loss that redundancy inflicts on people, while at the same time ensuring that fired employees are re-trained to better fit the new market situation. In addition, before people even enter the workforce, the welfare state plays an important role by providing tuition-free education, which typically is designed to be of direct value to the companies that hire graduates and people with vocational qualifications.

This makes for what we could call "the golden triangle of flexicurity," consisting of flexible labor markets, training and re-training, and unemployment protection, as illustrated in Figure 5.5. Together, these three elements form a specific logic whereby the welfare state facilitates the profit-making activities of trade and industry. Other aspects of the welfare state are less valuable to companies. Examples are early retirement schemes and disability pensions, which many Nordic company owners would probably like to see curtailed or abolished. Still, the flexicurity system helps to explain how businesses are able to survive and even thrive in the Nordics.

Figure 5.5 The golden triangle of flexicurity

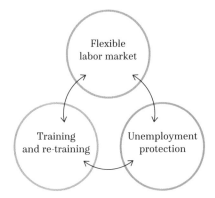

7.
For research documenting the positive effects of a business-friendly environment and economic growth, see Justesen (2008)

Another reason why businesses do well in the Nordics is the region's business-friendly environment.[7] Every year, the World Bank releases an Ease of Doing Business Index, which ranks countries according to how conducive their regulatory environment is to establishing and running a company there. The index is based on information about how long it takes and how much it costs to legally start a company, and how easy it is to get construction permits, to register property, and to pay taxes (since in some countries, even the US, this is remarkably difficult). In short, how bad is the bureaucracy?

In 2020, Denmark, Norway, and Sweden came in fourth, ninth, and tenth, respectively, on the Ease of Doing Business Index. Although the year-on-year rankings fluctuate a little, there is no doubt that the Nordics are at the absolute forefront when it comes to setting up a business. Once again, it is important to note that this does not imply that equality is somehow intrinsically good for a country's commercial climate. For instance, the US is number six on the list, while Singapore – another country with strong free-market credentials and sizeable inequalities – comes in second. Italy, on the other hand, is number 58, way down on the list along with Mexico and Kenya. The bottom line is, quite simply, that there is no direct link between equality and bureaucracy.

The third and final aspect I will highlight here is social trust.[8] People from the Nordic countries are among the most trusting in the world, with a majority of their populations agreeing with survey statements such as "people can usually be trusted." Social trust can be important for growth because it makes cooperation between individual citizens and companies easier. It is said to lower the transaction costs of a country's economy; something that, in turn, increases the willingness of entrepreneurs and banks to invest in that economy. By contrast, in countries with low levels of social trust, operating a business

8.
For research documenting the positive relationship between social trust and economic growth, see, e.g., Zak & Knack (2001) and Horváth (2013)

requires a lot of monitoring of employees (Do they do the job as you instructed them to?), other firms (Do they deliver the goods on time, and in the agreed condition?), and consumers (Will they pay on time?). Nordic businesses can take the liberty of spending less time and money on these sorts of monitoring activities and, instead, focus on producing and selling their goods and services.

Chapter 6.
The self-reinforcing nature of Nordic equality

The Nordic model of equality not only affects the economy; it has political implications too. More specifically, it creates powerful *feedback effects* that reinforce egalitarian outcomes: The fact that the less well-off are not too far below the middle class means that they are not regarded as alienated from the rest of society, which, in turn, makes it more likely that the middle class will support redistribution policies. The transparency of the universal welfare state means that taxpayers understand how their tax money is spent, which increases acceptance of a heavy tax burden. What is more, high levels of economic equality push up voter turnout among the less well-off, which creates an electoral market for parties representing this group. Finally, high levels of gender equality have ensured that women are better represented in the political system, creating a knock-on effect and promoting women-friendly policies. Taken together, these feedback effects profoundly influence the way politics play out in the Nordics.

"Deservingness"

As outlined in Chapter 2, the Nordic welfare state model is universal. This means that everyone has the right, as needed, to access the same public benefits and services, which are paid for and organized by the government. However, the universal welfare state does more than that; it affects how *deserving* the country's citizens think welfare claimants are – which has substantial political ramifications (Rothstein 1998; van Oorschot 2000; Larsen & Dejgaard 2013).

The main alternative to the universal welfare state is a means-tested system. In what are known as "means-tested welfare states," such as the US, the UK, and Australia, only the poor are typically eligible for benefits, while the rest of the population have to pay their own way if they happen to lose their job or experience some other mishap. Thus, a key discussion in means-tested welfare states is where, exactly, the cut-off point should be between those who are poor enough to get benefits and those who need to fend for themselves. It goes without saying that this gives people who earn too much money to qualify for benefits an incentive to think that, generally speaking, too many people are receiving benefits that are too generous. Since the cut-off point in means-tested benefit programs is typically rather low – because the benefits are only meant for the poorest citizens – this tends to pit the middle class (who will never receive any of the benefits, but who must pay for them through taxes) against the less well-off (who are more likely to qualify). In countries where many benefits are means-tested, benefit claimants therefore quickly end up being framed as "different" from the citizens who make up mainstream society. Public discourse soon comes to focus on whether claimants are truly needy, or whether they are playing the system. Frequently, claimants are framed as lazy, or as cheaters who are effectively to blame for their own predicament.

In a universal welfare state such discourse is less prominent, since everyone has equal access to all benefits. At least in principle, benefit claimants are "everyone and anyone" and not just "them" – as in "the poor and marginalized," who live on the fringes of society. As a result, opinions about claimants are much more benign, due to the logic that if claimants are like you and me, they can't be all that bad. This positive view is strengthened by the fact that Scandinavian claimants *are*, as a matter of fact, very much like the average Dane, Swede, or Norwegian. This follows directly from the high levels of equality, where the distance from the bottom to the middle class is limited. The lifestyle of a person on unemployment benefits is not radically different from the lifestyle of a member of the middle class. This creates a social affinity – a sense of commonality – between the claimants and most other people in society, which rarely exists in means-tested welfare states. It therefore makes sense that benefit claimants in the Nordics are much more frequently portrayed as people who have simply been struck by misfortune or dealt a bad hand in life. This reduces much of the personal blame others tend to lay on them for their life situation.

In representative democracies, these diverse climates of public opinion affect policy-making. In universal welfare states, political parties will factor in the level of overall support for most benefits. Under normal circumstances, no parties – not even the fiscally conservative ones – will propose significant cuts to, say, unemployment benefits or old-age pensions. If they did, they would probably lose at the polls. As a result, the already high level of equality is maintained. Essentially, this relationship between the universal welfare state, equality, and public policies constitutes a feedback loop: Due to the high equality generated by the universal welfare state, support for the universal model remains high, which again helps to maintain high equality, and so on and so forth.

Transparency

The universal welfare state not only helps to build and maintain social affinity between the less well-off and the middle class. Due to its design, it also enjoys a sense of widespread legitimacy among the public: Taxpayers understand the connection between their tax bill and the welfare state, and they agree with the principles and processes by which it operates. This legitimacy leads to lasting support for the universal welfare state, initiating the feedback loop I just described, which underpins the Nordic model of equality.[9]

In the context of the welfare state's legitimacy, the key issue is *transparency*. As described in Chapter 2, the universal welfare states of the Nordic countries are based on general taxation of income and consumption. In return, taxpayers get free access to a wide range of benefits and services, including education for their children, care for their elderly parents, and healthcare when they become ill. The government provides almost everything directly. Schools are overwhelmingly state-run, as are hospitals, daycare institutions, and care homes. In this sense, the connection between taxes and welfare is clear and unambiguous. This does not mean that people living in the Nordics enjoy paying high taxes – presumably, no one in the world does. Rather, it means that most people appreciate that the arrangement gives them something valuable – a safety net if they lose their job, healthcare if they become ill, and education for their children – in return. If citizens failed to see that connection, support would drop significantly.

Another aspect of transparency that gives the welfare state legitimacy is found in the procedures by which access is granted to benefits and services. In means-tested

9.
For research on this topic, see, e.g., Rothstein (1998), Kumlin & Rothstein (2005), and Gingrich (2014)

welfare states, people typically need to undergo screening before they can be deemed eligible. Research suggests that people tend to lose faith in the system when they undergo screening (Kumlin & Rothstein 2005). This is presumably because they feel scrutinized, and also fear being treated unfairly. In addition, the wider public may grow suspicious of the system if they do not fully comprehend the rules that regulate access, which ordinary people rarely do. This can give rise to unjustified grievances about how easy it is to get benefits and – by implication – how undeserving the beneficiaries must be. At least in theory, most of these problems are avoided in a universal welfare state, precisely because people are automatically entitled to help if they need it.

Transparency is a crucial feature of the universal welfare state because it reduces public discontent. In countries like the US, the welfare system is often portrayed as one of the problems facing society, not as part of a solution. In the Nordics, the welfare state is embraced wholeheartedly. A vital reason for this is that a majority of people believe it works well and can be trusted. Needless to say, this is a hindrance to far-reaching reform, thereby keeping the existing social arrangements in place.

Voter turnout

A high turnout at elections is also significant, because the tendency of certain social groups *not* to vote is not random. It is a well-established fact that the more resources people have – the more money, education, and so on – the more likely they are to vote. More importantly, from the current perspective, economic inequality has been shown to amplify these resource-based discrepancies (Solt 2008). That is, the more unequal a society is, the more these resource levels affect whether citizens vote or not.

Based on these findings, the turnout numbers at the most recent national elections, displayed in Figure 6.1, are less surprising. The three Nordics, with their high levels of equality, also boast high levels of turnout: Around 85 percent of eligible voters showed up at the ballot boxes in Denmark and Sweden, while 78 percent cast their votes in Norway. In the US, a low-equality country, only around 66 percent voted in the 2020 presidential election. In fact, this number is high when compared to the previous presidential election in 2016, when only 56 percent voted, and to congressional midterm elections in general, where voter turnout is typically around 35 percent. With a turnout of 72 percent, Italy falls between the Nordics and the US, although with a declining trend. This points to another important fact: Turnout rates in the Nordics have remained remarkably stable for several decades, whereas in many other countries they have been declining.

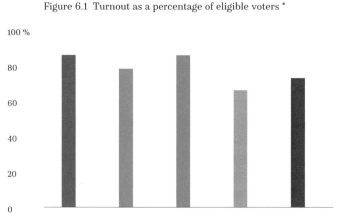

Figure 6.1 Turnout as a percentage of eligible voters *

* The elections reported are the most recent parliamentary elections, except for the US figure, which refers to the 2020 presidential election

Source: International Institute for Democracy and Electoral Assistance (2018)

62

Much would indicate that the high levels of equality found in the Nordics affect voter turnout, which is important because this, in turn, affects the political landscape, making it more likely that governments will pursue policies that secure the already high levels of equality. High turnout becomes part of a feedback mechanism that stabilizes the Nordic model of equality.[10]

10.
For research on the political role of turnout, see, e.g., Pacek & Radcliff (1995), Pontusson & Rueda (2010), and Bechtel et al. (2016)

In the mechanism's first stage, high turnout among the less well-off means that there is an electoral market for parties that seek to promote equality. If turnout is low, especially among their own target segments, parties representing these voters will have a much smaller likelihood of having politicians elected. Over time, such parties will either vanish or adapt their policy profile to better match the preferences of the people who actually show up to vote. This is arguably one reason why the Democrats in the US, who profess to be the more left-leaning of the two main parties, pursue policies that would be considered right-wing by Nordic standards. Conversely, when voter turnout is high, leftist parties tend to be more electorally successful and pursue more left-leaning policies.

In the Nordics, the largest left-wing parties have invariably been social democratic. These broad-based parties have frequently won around a third of the total vote, and sometimes much more. Importantly, the social democrats are never the only left-wing party in a given parliament. This creates political competition with the smaller leftist parties to win the votes of the less well-off. This not only enhances the likelihood that the left-wing parties will represent this segment of the electorate; it also means that these voters are more likely to turn out in the first place.

In the next stage, this particular electoral "market" influences which policies are implemented. Since the leftist parties tend to be successful in national elections, they will also come to wield governmental power relatively often – and when they do, they will already have committed themselves to pursuing egalitarian policies. Yet even outside government, strong leftist parties will often be able to put pressure on conservative governments, making it more difficult for them to pursue their first-order preferences of lower taxes and less economic equality.

In the third and final stage of the feedback mechanism, these egalitarian outcomes reinforce turnout. As already noted, this partly happens because the competition between various leftist parties will engage and mobilize the voters who are less well-off. Yet more importantly, because of the stronger presence of leftist parties in parliament, the egalitarian policies that originally helped foster high turnout rates will be maintained, and perhaps even expanded. This means that the resources of society's marginalized groups will continue to allow them to vote in similar numbers as before. The result is a virtuous circle between turnout and egalitarian policies.

Female representation

Formally, women and men are politically equal in all developed democracies, and people can vote and run for office regardless of gender. Given this, it is striking how varied the rate of female representation actually is in the political establishment. To get a sense of this, see Figure 6.2, which shows the percentage of seats in parliament occupied by women. In the Nordic countries, around 40 percent of all parliamentarians are female, compared to just over 35 percent in Italy and around 24 percent in the US (just below 24 percent in the House of Representatives, and 25 percent in the Senate).

Of course, women may be well-represented in parliament but hold little real power if they are kept away from the more influential positions. However, Nordic women also appear to be leading the way in this respect. Both Denmark and Norway have had women serve as prime ministers in recent years, and in all the Nordic countries women have held senior positions such as Minister of Foreign Affairs, Minister of Finance, and Minister of the Interior. It is, today, a conventional goal for incoming prime ministers to aim for gender parity in their cabinets, although that goal is not always achieved. For instance, as of 2021, the Danish government had only seven women among its 20 cabinet members.

* The US data is for the House of Representatives

Figure 6.2 Percentage of female representation *

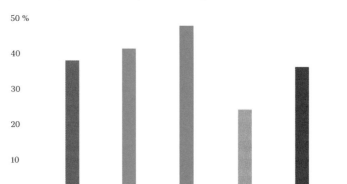

Source: The Inter-Parliamentary Union (2019)

The high levels of female representation arguably reflect a broader acceptance of gender equality in the Nordic countries (Paxton & Kunovich 2003), which is also manifested in the labor market, as explained in Chapter 3. Whatever the cause, research indicates that the effect of women in political representation is more women-friendly policies (Bolzendahl & Brooks 2007), that is, policies that further consolidate gender equality. This makes intuitive sense. Women politicians may be more acutely aware of the problems women face and therefore be more likely to put them on the political agenda. Over time, this has meant that more and more parties have adopted women-friendly policy positions. And this, in turn, has solidified a normative ideal of gender equality. Today, no Nordic politician would dare suggest that women are not entitled to enjoy the same social and political rights as their male peers.

Chapter 7.

The art of compromise

Political compromises are another important characteristic of the politics of equality in the Nordic countries. There is an argument to be made that the need to reach compromises has shaped the Nordic countries in a fundamental way, both in terms of the historical construction of the welfare state and labor market, and regarding the conduct of politics today. The end result is a political climate that is much less polarized than in, say, the US. By itself, this consensus-based approach to politics can help explain why citizens in the Nordic countries are less put off by politics and politicians than Americans and most other Europeans are. This, in turn, makes it easier for politicians to forge new compromises.

The electoral system

The electoral systems in all the Nordic countries and self-governing territories are characterized by proportional representation (PR). Although the PR system is not unique to these countries, it is still an important component in their cultures of political consensus. The key feature of PR is that the seat allocation in parliament roughly mirrors the popularity of parties as measured by their share of the popular vote. If a party gets 10 percent of the votes, it also ends up with around 10 percent of the seats in parliament. The main alternative to PR is a system known as "first past the post." Here, the party with the most votes in a given electoral district wins a seat in parliament, while all other parties end up with nothing. In short, all the votes for non-elected candidates are discounted.

The main difference between the PR and first-past-the-post systems is the size of the electoral district. In the latter system, there is only a single parliamentary seat up for grabs. This is why all candidates who win fewer votes than the front-runner get nothing: There can be only one winner. In PR systems, on the other hand, there are multiple seats per district, and, accordingly, the districts are larger than in the first-past-the-post system. Table 7.1 compares the logic of the two systems. In the first column, we see the vote share of each candidate. Party A is the most popular and gets 40 percent of all votes cast; party B gets 30 percent; and parties C and D get 20 and 10 percent, respectively. In the next column, we see how this translates into seats in the first-past-the-post system: Party A gets one seat, while the rest leave empty-handed. In this scenario, 60 percent of all votes have no influence and are wasted. The last column depicts a PR system with 10 seats per district. Here, each party wins exactly the number of seats corresponding to its respective vote share. This means that zero percent of the votes are wasted.

Table 7.1 A stylized example translating votes into seats

	Vote share	Seat share in a first-past-the-post, 1-seat system	Seat share in a PR system with 10-seat districts
Party A	40	1	4
Party B	30	0	3
Party C	20	0	2
Party D	10	0	1

The example in Table 7.1 is stylized. In reality, it is impossible to ensure that *no* votes are wasted. Even if the electoral district were to encompass the entire country, there would still exist a threshold for winning a seat: If parliament has, say, 200 seats, a party would need 0.5 percent of all votes, as a minimum, to earn a seat (200/100 = 0.5). Still, the correlation between how people actually vote and the size of parties when they earn representation in parliament is much higher in PR systems than in first-past-the-post systems. For instance, in the UK general election in 2019, the Conservatives managed to get an absolute majority in parliament based on 43 percent of the popular vote – a degree of disproportionality that is the norm in the UK, but unheard of in countries with PR systems.[11]

11.
For a discussion of these issues, see Lijphart (2012)

As a result of their electoral system, the Nordic countries and territories have many parties in their legislative assemblies. In Norway and Sweden, there are currently eight parties in parliament, while there are nine in Denmark. The party system in all three Scandinavian countries is roughly the same. The center-left is dominated by a large social democratic party, which is typically the largest in parliament, harvesting 25–30 percent of all votes. To the left of the social democrats, there are one or two small socialist or green parties. On the center-right are usually a couple of conservative and free-market liberal parties. On the far right, we find the new populist parties: the Danish People's Party in Denmark, the Progress Party in Norway, and the Sweden Democrats in Sweden. Finally, between the two blocs of parties we often find various small centrist parties.

Because of the fragmented nature of Nordic party systems, forming a government is much trickier than in a first-past-the-post system, where a single party normally emerges with an absolute majority. Governments in the Nordics are frequently made up of a coalition of several parties that may not even have a parliamentary majority. In fact, such "minority governments" are quite common. Typically, however, they have a permanent support party backing them, making them much more stable than one might initially expect. Indeed, although the process of forming a government can be messy, once it is completed, a government will normally last for the entire election period.

Given the Nordic electoral system and the resulting make-up of parliaments and governments in this region, it is no surprise that compromises are an essential mechanism for getting anything done. No party is in a position to force through legislation on its own. This makes consensus-based politics a fact of life that is especially true because, historically, the small centrist parties – being in a position to shift from center-left to center-right – have often acted as political kingmakers. This dynamic has created a gravitational pull towards the middle ground, as the large parties on either side of the aisle have had to accommodate their small but strategically significant neighbors.

From the perspective of equality, the main consequence of this politics of compromise is the all-encompassing universal welfare states found in the Nordics. Although the labor movement has historically been very strong in the Nordic countries – with big social democratic parties and unions – the electoral system has meant that it never could decide policies on its own. The labor movement could set the agenda, but not dictate policy. This meant that it could not pursue policies that only benefitted its own voters – not least in the form of welfare benefits aimed at helping workers. To establish a parliamentary majority in favor of expanding the welfare state, the voters of other parties had to be included as well. This fostered a distinct logic: To secure protection for the workers, the social democrats endorsed a universal welfare state that encompassed all citizens (Esping-Andersen 1985; Korpi & Palme 1998). I will elaborate on this point below.

Corporatism

Another central feature that helps to foster a political culture of compromise is corporatism, which is defined as "the institutionalized and privileged integration of organized interests in the preparation and/or implementation of public policies" (Christiansen et al. 2010: 26). Corporatism is a mode of policy-making that ensures the inclusion of different social groups as "actors" in the decision-making process. Because this inclusion is institutionalized, corporatism often produces a consensus-based approach to politics: All actors know they will also need to negotiate with each other in the future, which makes compromises easier to reach.

In the Nordics, corporatism has been prevalent at least since World War II, but arguably it already played a role around the turn of the twentieth century (Christiansen 2017). In the context of equality, corporatism in labor market policy is especially significant. Here, unions representing employees and employer associations representing business have developed closely coordinated procedures for negotiating wages, working hours, and so on. As a result, several characteristics of the Nordic model of equality are, in fact, not legislation at all, but deals made and enforced by the unions and the employers' associations. In many instances, the rules spelled out in these deals are supplemented with laws passed by parliament, creating a complex legal web that obscures the boundaries between the actions and responsibilities of the unions and employers' associations on the one hand, and those of the state on the other.

Corporatism is not limited to politics at a national level; it matters for the everyday operation of businesses too. Many companies have union representatives that act as "shop stewards," intermediary links between individual employees and employers. This serves to protect employees, because employers are forced to interact with the employee via a union representative who is often well-versed in the rules, and who enjoys special protection (union representatives are typically very difficult to fire, making them less vulnerable to pressure from the management). On the other hand, company-level negotiations between employers and employees are made easier because the employers only need to talk to one or a few representatives, rather than talking to each employee individually. In principle, if not always in practice, this flexibility can benefit employers too.

All in all, corporatism – like the electoral system – has created a culture of compromise, where neither the employers nor the employees dominate in mutual interaction. This outcome is in stark contrast to the situation in, for instance, the US, where employers normally confront employees individually, and where collective bargains of the sort found in the Nordics are off the table. Put differently, the alternative to corporatism is almost always unfettered free market capitalism. As such, corporatism has helped bring about the high level of equality found in the Nordics. What is more, because of the institutionalized integration of unions, in particular, into the decision-making process, corporatism also means that radical reform proposals increasing inequality are less likely to be successful.

Compromises in Nordic history

The history of the Nordic region is full of compromises between opposing political forces, and these compromises have shaped the Nordic model of equality. To see what this means more specifically, I will investigate four key moments in the history of my own country. These Danish examples resonate strongly with the experiences of both Norway and Sweden.

The first key moment occurred in 1899 in the midst of the longest-ever labor market conflict in Denmark, which lasted for almost six months. At one point the conflict had escalated to the extent that it encompassed half of the entire workforce, with huge disruptive consequences for the affected companies (which could make no profit) and the employees (who had to go without pay). Neither side would yield to the other; both sides felt that the conflict was of vital importance, as a matter of principle. Finally, the resources on both sides were so severely depleted that they were forced to enter a compromise: the September Compromise of 1899. This agreement constitutes the cornerstone of corporatism in Denmark. In it, the two sides recognize each other's right to organize, and they agree that future disagreements should be settled according to a set of rules, preventing the sort of all-out conflict that occurred in 1899. Subsequent decades saw new rules added to the agreement, gradually forming the dense network of guidelines and norms for labor market negotiations that still largely applies today.

The second key moment, occurring in 1933, was the so-called Kanslergade Compromise. Once again the backdrop was a severe crisis, this time in the wake of the Great Depression. Unemployment rates had been soaring across the Western world since 1929, also hitting Denmark hard. The government, led by social democrats, wanted to create more public jobs and expand social protection, but it was blocked by the center-right, which commanded a majority in the second chamber of the then bicameral system. At the same time, Danish farmers experienced substantial hardship because exports, especially to the UK, their largest market, had dropped. Together, these proved to be the necessary ingredients for a compromise: The center-left got a substantial expansion of the welfare state, while the center-right got a devaluation of the Danish *krone*, boosting exports to the UK. The Kanslergade Compromise has since been heralded as the birth of the Danish welfare state. Although that is probably a slightly exaggerated assessment, it nevertheless points to the crucial importance of this particular compromise.

The third key moment was the introduction of the People's Pension (*folkepensionen*) in 1956. Making the existing but meagre old-age pension more generous had been a priority for the Social Democrats since 1945, at least. Originally, the party's plan had been to focus on the needs of poorer citizens in Denmark (read: social democratic voters). However, under the influence of the *Radikale Venstre* – a small centrist party and a frequent kingmaker in Danish politics – the Social Democrats were pushed in the direction of a universal pension program, that is, a fixed basic pension for all citizens, regardless of their financial means and funded through general taxes. Eventually, this idea also came to be accepted by the center-right parties, presumably due to a cynical logic: We cannot stop the center-left from introducing their idea, so we might as well make sure our voters benefit too. It is only a slight stretch to say that the universal welfare state – at least in the form of a uniform old-age pension – came about as a classic compromise: The strong Social Democrats obtained better protection for the party's voters, but this came at the price of including the voters of all the other parties as well. The end result was an extremely popular pension program that has been almost impossible to retrench since then.

The fourth and final key moment relates to this last point. In the Nordic model of equality, cutbacks to the welfare state are electorally dangerous for politicians. Most voters are strong supporters of the universal welfare state and want to keep it as it is, or even expand it. Any parties proposing cuts are therefore likely to lose votes to the parties that do not want cuts. Consequently, some of the most significant cutbacks are introduced as broad, cross-partisan compromises between the center-left and center-right. In this way, voters have nowhere to go with their frustration, because all the main parties are part of the deal. This is what happened in 2006, for instance, when the Danish retirement age was raised by two years and indexed to the living age, meaning that the retirement age will continue to rise as people get older on average. The reform made fiscal sense, and it has helped secure the old-age pension system for the future. However, it was also one of the largest cuts in the history of the Danish welfare state. Importantly, it was passed by the then center-right government together with the Social Democrats, and dissatisfied voters only had the far-left parties to turn to.

Chapter 8.

The deep historical roots of Nordic equality

To explain the success of the Nordics we need to take a step back, to consider the deeply rooted historical pre-conditions for the Nordic model of equality. Features such as political compromises, PR electoral systems, and corporatism are not enough to convey the full picture. There are two general factors of particular importance. The first is the lack of any ethno-religious conflict line in the Nordic countries. The Danish, Norwegian, and Swedish populations are highly homogenous in terms of language and religion. This makes it much easier to establish a large, redistributive welfare state, because everybody feels they belong to the same group.

The second feature is strong civil movements. These broad-based movements often morphed into the parties that dominated decision-making in the twentieth century. As a result, government was never captured by an elitist bureaucracy, which may have cared less about the problems of ordinary citizens. Because of their civil-movement origins, most Nordic parties also had an intuitive acceptance of the corporatist model, in which interest groups negotiated with each other.

Ethno-religious homogeneity

There are several reasons why religion and language have been relatively unimportant in the history of the Nordics. The first and most straightforward is the misfortune of war. Denmark and Sweden have both had large, multi-national kingdoms. Denmark was once the dominant power in the Baltic region, ruling Norway and large parts of northern Germany for centuries. Over time these dominions fell away, and by 1864, the year of a brief but bloody border war with Prussia, only the heartland and a few overseas territories were left. Although the country recouped some of its north German territory after a referendum there in 1920, the outcome was a small nation consisting exclusively of self-declared, protestant Danes. The trajectory of the Swedish decline is different from the Danish one, but the result is virtually identical. Having once been a major European empire, by the early twentieth century Sweden had been reduced to its current borders.

An additional factor was the Reformation in the early sixteenth century. The Danish and Swedish kings, and with them their citizens, adopted Protestantism, effectively curtailing the political power of the Church. Many monasteries were closed down, and church-owned land was taken over by the Crown. The clergy became civil servants, part of the hierarchy of the state, rather than belonging to the international Catholic Church. The fact that the new state churches were no longer an independent political force meant that religion never again became a serious political issue.

The lack of ethno-religious conflicts also meant that the Scandinavian labor movements were able to form into a single, coherent force in their countries more easily than elsewhere (van Kersbergen & Manow 2009). This was key to the evolution of the welfare state in the twentieth century. In countries where several nationalities or religions lived side by side, as in Germany, the Netherlands, or the US, it often proved difficult to find enough common ground to bring workers together under the same organizational structure. At the end of the day, many workers identified more as, say, Protestants or Catholics than as workers. This, in turn, meant that labor movements became fragmented along ethno-religious lines, significantly reducing their overall political power.

Ethno-religious homogeneity also matters in a broader sense, beyond its role in the labor movements. Plenty of research documents that people's willingness to pay for welfare-state benefits depends on their feelings of affinity with the recipients.[12] If benefits are seen as being disproportionally paid out to individuals who do not belong to "my" group of people, then I will be much less likely to support those benefits. A powerful ethno-religious conflict line will, almost by definition, diminish the affinity among citizens, making it much harder to create political support for a generous welfare state. This is especially true for universal welfare states where benefits are given to everyone who happens to be a citizen. In countries with an ethno-religious conflict line, welfare state expansion often occurs solely in the form of personal insurance plans that people pay into, to ensure their own future benefits. This way they do not have to pay for the welfare of people from other groups. In short, it is no coincidence that universal welfare states are exclusively found in countries with originally homogenous populations.

12.
See, e.g., Alesina & Glaeser (2004)

Civil movements and the state

The ethno-religious homogeneity of the Nordic countries was significant not only for the labor movement, but also for other civil movements. Of particular importance is the agrarian movement. Both the agrarian and labor movements had social, economic, and political ambitions, with the relative weight of each shifting over time and evolving differently in the various Nordic countries. These movements created a broad, encompassing web of associations and clubs for their respective members. Work life, leisure time, politics – indeed, most of life's activities could take place within the realm of the movement with which a person was affiliated. The agricultural and labor movements became powerful political forces, each with their own parties in parliament to represent their interests. The labor movement had the Social Democrats, while the agrarian movements normally had two parties: one for smallholders and another for owners of large farms.

These civil-movement parties have been part and parcel of the building of the Nordic equality model for the simple reason that they had a very strong presence in the Nordic parliaments for most of the twentieth century. The most obvious consequence of this was the acceptance and use of corporatism. Corporatism, as described earlier, also entails institutionalized negotiations between the representatives of civil movements, which these political parties found more natural than parties that were not nested in such movements. Indeed, corporatism allowed civil-movement representatives to pursue a two-pronged strategy. They could either try to get their preferred policies passed by parliament, or they could address their concerns via corporatist negotiations (given that these negotiations often had to be acknowledged by parliament – which was much easier when the major corporatist actors agreed – and in many instances, parliamentary acknowledgment became nothing more than a rubber stamp). In short, the success of corporatism owes a lot to the fact that the actors engaged in corporatist negotiations often had substantial influence in parliament as well.

The legacy of the broad civil movements is visible to this day, although union membership rates are dropping, and the number of farmers has declined dramatically. Perhaps most strikingly, the Nordics have a high participation rate in all sorts of civil organizations. This is the heritage of a "culture of engagement" generated by the old, sweeping movements in their heyday, which now benefits a wellspring of social clubs and associations, ranging from sports to charities. To outside observers, this may appear surprising: an all-encompassing welfare state that provides all manner of services and benefits, but does not crowd out civil society. Research documents that *no* such crowding out is taking place (van Oorschot & Arts 2005), and one reason for this is presumably the legacy of the civil movements and the culture of engagement and participation they helped to foster.

Chapter 9.
Challenges ahead

Discussions about equality and the Nordics can all too quickly become one-sided, purely positive narratives. This is not surprising, since equality is indeed something the Nordics are good at promoting. Accordingly, if equality is an outcome you like, the Nordics will, by definition, have a lot for you to love. In the context of equality, they are probably the best available real-world cases of politically and economically sustainable equality.

Yet even when our focus is squarely on equality, all is not perfect. I have already touched upon some of the unresolved issues: Full economic equality has never been achieved (nor has it ever been the goal), and gender equality is still wanting. Now, I will turn to two other issues of special relevance for future challenges, namely the "age burden" and the rising number of foreign-born residents in the Nordic countries.

The former squeezes public budgets, as an increasingly large proportion of citizens will stop working and paying their usual income taxes, even while enjoying a variety of the welfare state's services and benefits. Consequently, the fiscal viability of the Nordic welfare state is in jeopardy. The rising number of foreign-born residents constitutes an economic and political problem. Economically, labor market participation rates are too low in this group, straining public budgets. Politically, foreign-born residents have become a hot topic, undermining the feeling of affinity between all citizens. As discussed in the preceding chapter, this has historically been one of the special components of the Nordic welfare state model, but it is now slowly eroding.

The age burden

Figure 9.1 gives a sense of what I and many others candidly call the "age burden." The figure shows the proportion of the population aged 65 years or more in 1970 and 2014, respectively (with the numbers for Denmark and Sweden referring to 2013). Comparing these two years, we see not only how much the proportion of elderly has increased but also the magnitude of the current problem. In 1970, the average age burden in the Nordic countries was 13 percent. Today, it has increased to 18 percent, and this number is expected to rise further in the future. The Italian situation is worse, with the percentage of older citizens having increased even more dramatically. The American situation is better, not least because of the steady influx of young immigrants to the US.

In short, the Nordics are not alone in facing a demographic age burden, but that obviously does not diminish the problem, which is multi-faceted. When people get old, they retire and begin relying more on healthcare and care services for the elderly. Retirement means that people no longer work and therefore pay less in taxes. Nordic retirees are also entitled to old-age pensions and various other age-related benefits. Also, people are tending to live longer, which, of course, is good news for them, but bad news for the public purse that has to pay for their pensions for a longer period of time. All Nordic countries have reformed their old-age pension systems to meet these challenges, but compared to the situation in the 1950s, 1960s, and 1970s, when many of the pension programs were introduced, it is undeniable that the fiscal burden associated with retired citizens has grown substantially.

Figure 9.1 People aged 65 years or more as a percentage of the population

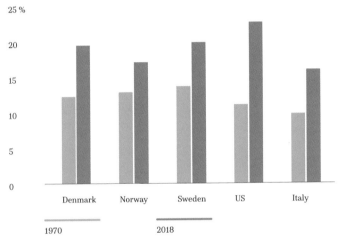

Source: OECD (2018)

Although people today live longer and healthier lives than ever before, with the onset of old age, people still start to rely more on healthcare and services for the elderly at some point. Typically, citizens become heavy users of public services during the last five years of their lives. With more people living longer, the volume of service users also increases. Healthcare, in particular, is extremely expensive, and health spending in all three Nordic countries has soared in recent years. With a rising number of elderly citizens, the costs of running nursing homes and the like are also increasing.

Figure 9.2 gives an impression of how much more is being spent to cover age-related issues. It reports, in US dollars, the spending per capita (per inhabitant) on benefits and services directly aimed at elderly citizens, plus healthcare services – which are predominantly (but not exclusively) used by the elderly. Because the numbers are adjusted for inflation, we can compare them directly across the two years. They are quite astounding, with the Nordic average having grown from $3,360 to $7,200 in three decades. When we compare Figures 9.1 and 9.2, it is easy to see how spending is rising at a faster pace than the percentage of elderly citizens. This reflects how benefits and services not only reach more people, but have also become more generous, or at least more expensive to provide.

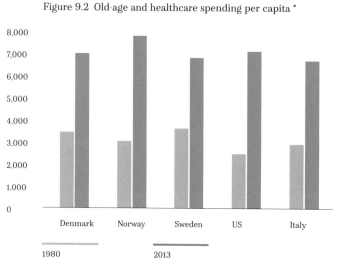

Figure 9.2 Old-age and healthcare spending per capita *

* Spending is measured as constant (adjusted for inflation) in US dollars

1980   2013

Source: OECD (2018)

86

It goes without saying that the sort of expansion we see in Figure 9.2 will, at some stage, force governments to act. Cutting generosity can be dangerous for politicians who want to be re-elected, so this avenue is mostly taken when the parties involved in such a compromise are able to share the blame, leaving voters nowhere to go. Alternatively, spending on the elderly segment will be allowed to keep increasing, while other public programs are cut.

Foreign-born residents

The second major problem facing the Nordic model of equality is the increasing number of foreign-born residents. Like other European countries, the Nordics have welcomed a large number of refugees and immigrants over the years, especially from the 1990s onwards. Exact and comparable historical statistics are hard to obtain, but the general increase is undisputable. Today, almost 20 percent of all Swedish inhabitants are foreign-born, with numbers somewhat lower in Denmark and Norway. This shift has caused both economic and political problems. The main economic problem relates to the low labor market participation of many non-natives, especially those from less-developed countries in Africa and the Middle East. Not only does the situation imply that too many new arrivals fail to contribute to the economy via their job; most of these jobless foreigners are also entitled to relatively generous benefits because of the universal welfare state.

Over time, the low labor market participation rates, combined with a rising fear of Islamism and terrorism, have created a great deal of antagonism between the native Danes, Norwegians, and Swedes, on the one hand, and the foreign-born residents and citizens on the other. One visible manifestation of this is the rise of far-right populist parties, which in Scandinavia are exemplified by the Danish People's Party, the Progress Party, and the Sweden Democrats. This phenomenon has, in turn, led the mainstream center-right parties to adopt much stricter positions on immigration. Policies have toughened markedly over the last few years, first in Denmark and then in Norway and Sweden.

As mentioned in the preceding chapter, ethno-religious homogeneity was an important precondition for the rise and realization of the Nordic model of equality. Letting everyone have a share of the welfare-state pie requires that the majority of citizens feel a minimum of social affinity with the people benefitting from the welfare state. With increasing antagonism, that affinity is disappearing fast. In Denmark, for instance, a majority has emerged that think newcomers should *not* have socio-economic benefits similar to those native Danes receive (Arndt & Jensen 2017). Some welfare programs have already been tailored to result in lower benefits for foreign-born citizens than for natives, a tendency that may well continue. Meanwhile, since many foreign-born residents are found among the most vulnerable socio-economic groups in Denmark, cutting their benefits is all but certain to create more inequality.

Chapter 10.
Conclusions

The Nordic countries are front-runners when it comes to equality, and they will probably maintain their prominent position in the coming years. In economic terms, the distances both from the poor to the middle class and from the middle class to the upper middle class are very short, measured by international standards. The reasons for this lie in a combination of how people earn a living and how the government taxes and spends. First, wages are decided collectively, leaving little room for individual wage negotiations between individual employees (whether talented or substandard) and their employers. Second, the universal welfare state ensures that low-income individuals have access to the same benefits and services as those with higher incomes (who have to pay disproportionately more in tax). This, too, reduces inequalities.

However, the most defining feature of the Nordic countries is not their economic equality; it is their gender equality. A large share of Nordic women earn their own money, and they are, in this sense, financially independent of their families. It has required a unique mix of policies – and a lot of public spending – to create the level of de-familization that characterizes the Nordics today, and female participation in the workforce is likely to remain high. The policy centerpiece here is the comprehensive childcare arrangements that allow women to balance work and family life. In combination with generous parental leave programs, this means that having children is less disruptive to women's work lives than it is elsewhere.

One of the primary tenets of the Nordic model of equality is low intergenerational inequality. Although Nordic young people are exposed to some of the same risks as youth everywhere else, large-scale investment in tuition-free, high-quality education for all segments of society, combined with flexible labor markets, makes their situation much more tolerable. Young people in the Nordic countries relatively rarely end up in the NEET statistics – which reflect those who are "not in education, employment, or training" – and a large proportion of children from families with less-educated parents end up with a college-level degree. This trend is stable, and governments are also making efforts to promote life-long learning and offer retraining programs for older adults as labor markets change.

An oft-heard truism states that equality and economic growth must necessarily be mutually exclusive. This is plainly wrong. Obviously, the Nordics are a prime example that the two can coexist. For this particular set of countries, the features that have "kept the bumblebee flying" are their unique flexicurity systems, a business-friendly environment with comparatively little bureaucracy, and high levels of social trust. Taken together, these features have made it possible for Nordic businesses to stay profitable, and in light of their success, this strategy is hardly likely to change much in the foreseeable future.

A set of powerful feedback effects upholds the Nordic model of equality. Together, they make it very difficult politically to introduce radical reforms to the model. The high levels of equality mean that benefit claimants are normally not considered as outsiders, but rather as part of the social mainstream. This general acceptance creates a social affinity between the politically important middle class and the more marginalized groups, a feeling that is enhanced by the fact that the universal welfare state, by design, includes the entire population. From a welfare-state perspective, there are no outsiders. High equality also increases voter turnout among the less well-off, forcing the political parties to take their concerns seriously. A similar logic reigns when it comes to female political representation: More begets more. In this way, extensive gender equality leads to better representation, which in turn leads to more women-friendly policies and, hence, more gender equality further down the road.

The culture of compromise that characterizes Nordic politics has been vital, both in creating the conditions under which the high levels of equality could come about in the first place, and in upholding this equality later on. Multi-party coalitions, which are routinely necessary to govern in the region's various assemblies, tend to hinder radical reforms and pull parties towards the center. Similarly, corporatism means that the representatives of employers and employees have become accustomed to negotiating with each other, which also promotes and sustains a consensus culture. In both instances, the result is a depolarized political climate, which has made it easier to maintain the Nordic model of equality.

There is a certain irony in the fact that the Nordic model of equality largely owes its success to the many historical defeats Denmark and Sweden have suffered, which, in Scandinavia, carved out three ethno-religiously homogenous populations. In combination with a weak Church, this meant that ethno-religious issues have been more or less off the table in Nordic politics, at least until recently. The populations' homogeneity was instrumental for the emergence of strong civil movements in general, and for a unified labor movement in particular. Without these, in all likelihood there would have been no Nordic model of equality.

Looking ahead, the Nordics face some stiff challenges. The two major ones both relate to the fiscal sustainability of the Nordic model of equality. With the numbers of elderly people and jobless foreign-born residents rising, the Nordic countries have less money to spend on everything else. Importantly, the need to prioritize has political ramifications. Non-natives are increasingly viewed as costly and undeserving of the help they receive. This contrasts dramatically with views on the elderly, whose benefits and services are all but sacrosanct. For many people living in the Nordics, a trade-off is coming into view between welfare for foreigners and welfare for the elderly. This only makes dissatisfaction with foreign-born residents worse, further eroding social affinity. The Nordic model has undeniably been a huge success from the perspective of equality. Nevertheless, arguably the success story so far has been the easy part, and the challenges now facing the three Scandinavian countries, and the Nordic region in general, are far more serious than anything they have previously overcome.

Suggestions for further reading

Esping-Andersen, G. (1999). *Social foundations of postindustrial economies*. Oxford University Press.

Jensen, C. & van Kersbergen, K. (2017). *The Politics of Inequality*. Palgrave.

OECD (2010). *Divided We Stand: Why Inequality Keeps Rising*. OECD Publishing.

Korpi, W. & Palme, J. (1998). The paradox of redistribution and strategies of equality: Welfare state institutions, inequality, and poverty in the Western countries. *American sociological review*, 661-687.

Rothstein, B. (1998). *Just institutions matter: The moral and political logic of the universal welfare state*. Cambridge University Press.

References

Alesina, A. & Glaeser, E. L. (2004). *Fighting poverty in the US and Europe: A world of difference*. Oxford University Press.

Arndt, C. & Jensen, C. (2017). Partivalg og holdninger til velfærdsstaten. In K. M. Hansen and R. Stubager (Eds.), *Oprør fra udkanten: Folketingsvalget 2015*. DJØF Publishers.

Bechtel, M. M., Hangartner, D., & Schmid, L. (2016). Does compulsory voting increase support for leftist policy? *American Journal of Political Science*, 60(3), 752-767.

Beramendi, P. & Rueda, D. (2007). Social democracy constrained: Indirect taxation in industrialized democracies. *British Journal of Political Science*, 37(4), 619-641.

Bolzendahl, C. & Brooks, C. (2007). Women's political representation and welfare state spending in 12 capitalist democracies. *Social Forces, 85*(4), 1509-1534.

Chevalier, T. (2016). Varieties of youth welfare citizenship: Towards a two-dimension typology. *Journal of European Social Policy, 26*(1), 3-19.

Christiansen, P. M. (2017). Still the corporatist darlings? In P. Nedergaard and A. Wivel (Eds.), *The Routledge Handbook of Scandinavian Politics.* Routledge.

Christiansen, P. M., Nørgaard, A. S., Rommetvedt, H., Svensson, T., Thesen, G., & Öberg, P. (2010). Varieties of democracy: Interest groups and corporatist committees in Scandinavian policy making. *Voluntas: International Journal of Voluntary and Nonprofit Organizations, 21*(1), 22-40.

Credit Suisse (2016). *Global Wealth Databook 2016.*

Cusack, T. R. & Beramendi, P. (2006). Wage-setting institutions and pay inequality in advanced industrial societies. *European Journal of Political Research, 45*(1), 43-73.

Esping-Andersen, G. (1985). *States against Markets.* Princeton University Press.

Esping-Andersen, G. (1990). *The Three Worlds of Welfare Capitalism.* Princeton University Press.

Esping-Andersen, G. (1999). *Social foundations of postindustrial economies.* Oxford University Press.

European Institute for Gender Equality (2018). *Gender Equality Index.* http://eige.europa.eu/gender-equality-index

Financial Times (2017, November 13). Italian emigration continues despite strong economic recovery.

Forbes Magazine (2018, March 8). The 25 countries with the most billionaires.

Gingrich, J. (2014). Visibility, values, and voters: The informational role of the welfare state. *The Journal of Politics, 76*(2), 565-580.

Gupta, N. D., Smith, N., & Verner, M. (2008). The impact of Nordic countries' family friendly policies on employment, wages, and children. *Review of Economics of the Household, 6*(1), 65–89.

Horváth, R. (2013). Does trust promote growth? *Journal of Comparative Economics, 41*(3), 777–788.

International Institute for Democracy and Electoral Assistance (2018). *Voter Turnout Database.* https://www.idea.int/data-tools/data/voter-turnout

Inter-Parliamentary Union (2019). *Women in National Parliaments.* http://archive.ipu.org/wmn-e/classif.htm

Iversen, T. & Stephens, J. D. (2008). Partisan politics, the welfare state, and three worlds of human capital formation. *Comparative Political Studies, 41*(4–5), 600–637.

Jensen, C. (2008). Worlds of welfare services and transfers. *Journal of European Social Policy, 18*(2), 151–162.

Jensen, C. & van Kersbergen, K. (2017). *The Politics of Inequality.* Palgrave.

Justesen, M. K. (2008). The effect of economic freedom on growth revisited: New evidence on causality from a panel of countries 1970–1999. *European journal of political economy, 24*(3), 642–660.

Korpi, W. & Palme, J. (1998). The paradox of redistribution and strategies of equality: Welfare state institutions, inequality, and poverty in the Western countries. *American sociological review,* 661–687.

Korpi, W., Ferrarini, T., & Englund, S. (2013). Women's opportunities under different family policy constellations: Gender, class, and inequality tradeoffs in western countries re-examined. *Social Politics: International Studies in Gender, State & Society, 20*(1), 1–40.

Kumlin, S. & Rothstein, B. (2005). Making and breaking social capital: The impact of welfare-state institutions. *Comparative political studies, 38*(4), 339–365.

Kvist, J., Fritzell, J., Hvinden, B., & Kangas, O. (2012). *Changing Social Equality: The Nordic welfare model in the 21st century.* Policy Press.

Larsen, C. A. & Dejgaard, T. E. (2013). The institutional logic of images of the poor and welfare recipients: A comparative study of British, Swedish and Danish newspapers. *Journal of European Social Policy, 23*(3), 287–299.

Lewis, J. (1992). Gender and the development of welfare regimes. *Journal of European Social Policy, 2*(3), 159–173.

Lijphart, A. (2012). *Patterns of democracy: Government forms and performance in thirty-six countries.* Yale University Press.

Lohmann, H. & Zagel, H. (2016). Family policy in comparative perspective: The concepts and measurement of familization and defamilization. *Journal of European Social Policy, 26*(1), 48–65.

Mandel, H. & Semyonov, M. (2005). Family policies, wage structures, and gender gaps: Sources of earnings inequality in 20 countries. *American sociological review, 70*(6), 949–967.

Mandel, H. & Semyonov, M. (2006). A welfare state paradox: State interventions and women's employment opportunities in 22 countries. *American journal of sociology, 111*(6), 1910–1949.

Neves, P. C., Afonso, Ó., & Silva, S. T. (2016). A meta-analytic reassessment of the effects of inequality on growth. *World Development, 78*, 386–400.

OECD (2016). *Society at a Glance 2016.* OECD Publishing.

OECD (2017). *Education at a Glance 2017.* OECD Publishing.

OECD (2018). *OECD Stats.* http://stats.oecd.org/

Pacek, A. & Radcliff, B. (1995). Turnout and the vote for left-of-centre parties: A cross-national analysis. *British Journal of Political Science, 25*(1), 137–143.

Paxton, P. & Kunovich, S. (2003). Women's political representation: The importance of ideology. *Social Forces, 82*(1), 87–113.

Pontusson, J. & Rueda, D. (2010). The politics of inequality: Voter mobilization and left parties in advanced industrial states. *Comparative Political Studies, 43*(6), 675-705.

Rothstein, B. (1998). *Just institutions matter: the moral and political logic of the universal welfare state.* Cambridge University Press.

Solt, F. (2008). Economic inequality and democratic political engagement. *American Journal of Political Science, 52*(1), 48-60.

Statistics Denmark (2015). *Færre børn i daginstitutionerne efter skolereformen.* www.dst.dk/nyt/19245

Thewissen, S. (2014). Is it the income distribution or redistribution that affects growth? *Socio-Economic Review, 12*(3), 545-571.

Van Kersbergen, K. & Manow, P. (Eds.). (2009). *Religion, class coalitions, and welfare states.* Cambridge University Press.

Van Oorschot, W. & Arts, W. (2005). The social capital of European welfare states: The crowding out hypothesis revisited. *Journal of European social policy, 15*(1), 5-26.

Van Oorschot, W. V. (2000). Who should get what, and why? On deservingness criteria and the conditionality of solidarity among the public. *Policy & Politics, 28*(1), 33-48.

Visser, J. & Checchi, D. (2009). Inequality and the Labor Market: Unions. In *The Oxford Handbook of Economic Inequality.* Oxford University Press.

Wallerstein, M. (1999). Wage-setting institutions and pay inequality in advanced industrial societies. *American Journal of Political Science, 43*(3), 649-680.

Zak, P. J. & Knack, S. (2001). Trust and growth. *The Economic Journal, 111*(470), 295-321.